Relational Leadership Development: An Ethnological Study in Inuit Contexts

Enoch Wan & John Ferch

Relational Paradigm Series of CDRR

*Relational Leadership Development:
An Ethnological Study in Inuit Contexts*

Enoch Wan & John Ferch

Copyright 2022 © Western Academic Publishers

Cover designed by Mark Benec

ISBN: 978-1-954692-07-7

All rights reserved. Except for brief quotations in critical publications or reviews, no part of this book may be reproduced in any manner without prior written permission from the publisher or author.

"Scripture quotations are from The ESV® Bible (The Holy Bible, English Standard Version®), copyright © 2001 by Crossway, a publishing ministry of Good News Publishers. Used by permission. All rights reserved.".

CDRR (Center of Diaspora & Relational Research) @
https://www.westernseminary.edu/outreach/center-diaspora-relational-research

Western Academic Publishers

Table of Contents

CHAPTER 1 INTRODUCTION   1
    THE BACKGROUND OF THIS BOOK 1
    BACKGROUND OF THE CO-AUTHORS 1
    THE PURPOSES OF THIS BOOK 2
    THE READERSHIP OF THIS BOOK 3
    DEFINITION OF KEY TERMS 3
    THE ORGANIZATION OF THIS BOOK 4

CHAPTER 2 BACKGROUND KNOWLEDGE   5
    INTRODUCTION 5
    LEADERSHIP DEVELOPMENT IN THE FAR NORTH 5
    WORLDVIEW STUDIES 10
    THE "GLOCAL" APPROACH 19
    SUMMARY 21

CHAPTER 3 OVERVIEW OF LEADERSHIP DEVELOPMENT PROGRAMS   23
    INTRODUCTION 23
    GREENLAND 23
    ALASKA 28
    CANADA 47
    SUMMARY 50

CHAPTER 4 ETHNOLOGY OF INUIT LEADERSHIP DEVELOPMENT   53
    INTRODUCTION 53
    INUIT PATTERNS OF EDUCATION 53
    INUIT PATTERNS OF LEADERSHIP 65
    INUIT PATTERNS OF SOCIAL CONTROL 71
    SUMMARY 84

CHAPTER 5 RELATIONAL LEADERSHIP DEVELOPMENT   87
    INTRODUCTION 87
    CHRISTIAN TRANSFORMATIVE LEARNING THEORY 87

 Relational Leadership Theory 91
 Honor–Shame Theory 95
 Towards a Relational Model 99
 Summary 106
CHAPTER 6 ORALITY-BASED LEADERSHIP DEVELOPMENT   109
 Introduction 109
 Orality-based Pedagogy 110
 Narrative-based Curriculum 113
 Summary 123
CHAPTER 7 AN INTEGRATED MODEL FOR INUIT MINISTRY LEADERSHIP DEVELOPMENT   125
 Recommendations for Further Study 127
 Broader Missiological Implications 128
APPENDIX 1 RESEARCH DESIGN: DATA COLLECTION AND DATA ANALYSIS   129
 Methodological Design 129
 Research Process & Procedures 129
 Technique 130
 Summary 130
BIBLIOGRAPHY   131

Chapter 1
Introduction

The Background of this Book

John Ferch conducted archival research, by (a) collecting ethnographic literature pertaining to circumpolar Inuit culture, and (b) gathering information on existing ministry leadership development programs serving Inuit people in his doctoral studies, under the supervision of Enoch Wan. The two then spent months on the book project, leading to publication of this volume in 2021.

Background of the Co-authors

Enoch Wan

Enoch Wan has served on the faculty at Western Seminary for twenty years, giving leadership to the two doctoral programs in intercultural studies and intercultural education. He served for two terms as president of the Evangelical Missiological Society and as VP in various capacities for two decades. For more than a decade, he launched studies in diaspora missiology and relational paradigm with publications of books and articles along these two themes.

John Ferch

I was raised as an MK in New Tribes Mission (today Ethnos360), which serves indigenous people groups worldwide. My parents' first term overseas was spent in Greenland, where we lived in an Inuit community as part of a church planting team. I completed grades 1-4 in the Greenlandic public school system, experiencing first-hand some of the educational approaches described later in this study. My parents served a later term in Chihuahua, Mexico, where they held administrative roles to support indigenous church planting teams in several remote mountain villages. I "cut my teeth" in ministry as a teen working alongside volunteer work teams under the summer sun of the Chihuahuan desert, helping to build a Bible school for the training of indigenous ministers.

My later experiences in Bible college and seminary convinced me of the strategic importance of indigenous leadership development to the missiological task. Though I initially envisioned myself in a pioneer church planting role on the mission field, I became convicted about the lack of indigenous leadership in the global church. The training and resources that I enjoyed as a North American seminary graduate were in short supply around the world, and rather than investing this training in one new pioneer church plant myself, I realized that I could better steward these resources by multiplying indigenous leaders who could shepherd many indigenous church plants in their own cultures.

Upon graduation from seminary, my wife and I accepted a role at Alaska Bible College (ABC), which had been founded fifty years earlier to train leaders for the church in Alaska. I was eager to help train church leaders among the Inuit people that I had come to love through my time in Greenland as a child. ABC had long operated as a ministry of SEND International but had recently been given organizational independence and was seeking to reposition itself to increase its effectiveness in training Alaskan ministry leaders. Specifically, as Vice President for Academic Affairs, I was tasked to launch an online curriculum and to help lead the school's transition from a rural location to a newly acquired urban campus.

I took on this role with the optimistic and naïve idea that these changes would lead many aspiring young Alaska Native believers throughout the state to enroll at Alaska Bible College to be trained as leaders for their churches. If we were able to solve the problem of access to training by offering courses online and in urban centers, then Alaska's many indigenous churches could finally receive the indigenous leadership that was lacking.

Although the college did receive a boost in enrollment through these efforts, few came from Inuit or other Alaska Native backgrounds. Rather, it was predominantly Caucasian students that took advantage of the new online classes and the urban campus. During my tenure, no indigenous students from rural villages enrolled in online coursework, and though the new urban location did attract several Inuit students who may not have otherwise been interested, the demographic profile of the overall student population remained relatively unchanged.

Moreover, as I worked with these students in the classroom, I increasingly began to realize a disconnect between the traditional Western approach to theological education and the needs and expectations of these rural Inuit students. They tended to struggle academically in the classroom and culturally in the college environment. Few completed the entire academic program, and none of those that did graduate continued on the path to vocational ministry afterwards. I began to suspect that the traditional Bible college and seminary track was not an ideal model for leadership development among the Inuit.

The Purposes of this Book

The purpose of this book is to present a proposed relational, orality-based model for ministry leadership development that is "glocalized" to Inuit contexts, using comparative study of existing ethnographic data as the primary research method.

The Readership of this Book

This book is written for three kinds of readership: (1) Christian professionals who are working in the area of leadership development; (2) Christian leaders (e.g., pastors and missions executives, etc.) and trainers (e.g., faculty members of seminary & Bible school); (3) students of native culture and leadership study.

Definition of Key Terms

As we begin this endeavor, it is helpful to establish our meaning behind a few key words and phrases that are foundational to the task at hand. These terms set the stage for the discussion and assist us in comparing "apples to apples." They are listed here in alphabetical order.

Analytical Logic

An approach to understanding and interpreting reality through a series of propositional statements that form a systematic outline corresponding to reality. The scientific method, Aquinas' *Summa Theologica*, and systematic approaches to theology are examples of analytical logic.

Glocal

As opposed to "global" (one model fits all) and "local" (a unique model for each culture) approaches to education, a "glocal" approach is "designed for mixed audiences that comprise a 'multi-faceted cultural mosaic.'"[1]

Integrated Model

An approach to ministry leadership development that incorporates both relational and narrative logic into the discipleship process. This is contrasted against the Western analytical model because it approaches discipleship through a lens of relationships to be developed rather than curricular knowledge to be imparted, and correspondingly employs orality-based methods for teaching and learning.

Inuit

The related ethnolinguistic people groups inhabiting the Arctic coastlines of eastern Siberia, Alaska, Canada, and Greenland, as represented by the Inuit Circumpolar Council.

Ministry Leadership Development

The discipleship of mature believers for Christian service in the church. This

---

[1] Tom Steffen, *Worldview-based Storying: The Integration of Symbol, Story, and Ritual in the Orality Movement* (Richmond: Orality Resources International, 2018). 216.

includes both "vocational" leaders (who receive formal recognition for their efforts, often in the form of financial compensation) and "lay" leaders (who may go without formal recognition).

Narrative Logic

As opposed to analytical logic, narrative logic is an approach to understanding and interpreting reality through stories, which provide a narrative grid or "metanarrative" that explains the world and makes sense of reality.

Orality

"Orality (oral, aural, visual, digital, social) denotes pedagogical preferences designed to process, remember, and communicate verbally and pictorially through social connections, rather than through literate forms."[2]

Relational Logic

The understanding that reality is experienced and interpreted through relational networks, including "vertical" relationships with God and "horizontal" relationships within the created order.[3]

The Organization of this Book

This book begins with a general introduction (chapter 1) and ends with a proposed integrated model for Inuit ministry leadership development (chapter 7). Readers are provided with background knowledge of leadership development, worldview studies and "glocal" approach in chapter 2. Chapter 3 is an overview of leadership development in Greenland, Alaska, and Canada. Chapter 4 is an ethnology of Inuit leadership development in terms of patterns of education, leadership, and social control. Chapter 5 is a theoretical overview of Christian transformative learning, relational leadership, and honor-shame. Chapter 6 introduces orality-based leadership development.

---

[2] Steffen, *Worldview-based Storying*, 29.
[3] Enoch Wan, "The Paradigm of 'Relational Realism,'" *EMS Occasional Bulletin*, vol. 19, no. 2 (Spring 2006), 1-4. 1; Paul G. Hiebert, *Transforming Worldviews: An Anthropological Understanding of How People Change* (Grand Rapids: Baker, 2008). 43.

Chapter 2
Background Knowledge

Introduction

Though we attempt in this book to "nudge" the church's indigenous leadership development efforts in new, more holistic and biblically-based directions, we are certainly not the first to the table! We stand on the shoulders of many who have gone before, both in terms of field experience and theoretical exercise. In the present chapter, we provide some of the theoretical or "academic" context for our study, tracing the key lines of thought that have influenced our own thinking on the matters at hand. We begin by exploring the importance of leadership development to the missiological task—both in general and in the Far North. We then outline some major anthropological concepts that inform our study, particularly surrounding the concept of "worldview." Finally, we establish the value of the "glocal" approach that we take in developing our integrated model.

Leadership Development in the Far North

Protestant missionaries have been evangelizing and planting churches in Inuit communities for over 300 years. Hans Egede established Lutheranism in Greenland under the Danish crown, and was closely followed by the Moravian community of "New Herrnhut." The Anglican church spread throughout northern Canada (again, with a Moravian presence in Newfoundland & Labrador). Sheldon Jackson, the "Apostle to Alaska," is credited with facilitating the "Comity Plan," in which major denominations (including the Moravians) were organized to focus their mission efforts in distinct areas of the territory without overlap.[4]

Over the years, missionaries have been quite successful in planting churches. Yet evangelism is not the end of the Great Commission, for the task is to make *disciples*, not merely *converts*. Though churches were established quite rapidly, today's Evangelical congregations remain largely dependent on missionary pastors.[5] Gary Ridley described this situation in Alaska in his account of a 1987 mission strategy meeting:

---

[4] J. Arthur Lazell, *Alaskan Apostle: The Life Story of Sheldon Jackson* (New York: Harper & Brothers, 1960), 65.
[5] Barry James Rempel, *An Action Research Exploration of Leadership Formation Among the Ahtna That Resulted in the Discovery of Factors Encouraging the Emergence of Indigenous Christian Leaders* (D.Min. product, Tyndale Seminary, 2014), 14.

In November of 1987 the writer attended a meeting of missionaries and concerned Native church leaders to discuss ways of meeting the training needs of young Native leaders. Five missionaries and four native leaders met informally at Victory Bible Camp for two days. Two of the missionaries serve with SEND International of Alaska, three serve with Interact Ministries (formerly Arctic Missions). The native leaders are involved in ministries founded by these two missions. Many who attended the meeting expressed concern that there were not a sufficient number of young Native leaders to replace the older ones who are dying off. In many Native communities the pastors and church leaders are in their sixties and seventies. Everyone at the meeting agreed that the need to train younger leaders for the Native church of the future is great.[6]

Not much has changed in thirty years. Barry Rempel recounts,

> a 2012 mission conference held in Anchorage listed Church Leadership Development as a workshop option. However, the workshop was cancelled because the two veteran missionaries slated to lead the discussion declared they had never seen sufficient leadership development take place in order to speak to the matter.[7]

In 2013-2014, I (John) served as a member of a Consultation Team that focused on the same questions that Gary Ridley faced in 1987. Six Caucasian missionaries and four Native leaders met on a monthly basis to assess the state of the Great Commission in Alaska and to identify the greatest areas of need. Organizations represented were Alaska Bible College, Alaska Freedom Journey, Arctic Barnabas, The Evangelical Covenant Church of Alaska, Hearts Going Toward Wellness, and InterAct Ministries. The unanimous conclusion of this Consultation Team was that the Alaska Native church still lacks mature indigenous leadership and that discipleship of such leaders is the key remaining task.[8]

Focusing on the global missionary effort as a whole, Tom Steffen has made a strong case that the Western church must phase out of what he calls the "pioneer" role of church planting and development.[9] He argues that since viable national churches now exist in every nation (though not every people group), these national churches have a responsibility to take up the cause of the Great

---

[6] Gary J. Ridley, *Leadership Development in Native Alaskan Churches: Teaching Biblical Leadership Principles in the Light of an Analysis of Traditional Patterns of Leadership* (D.Miss. product, Trinity Evangelical Divinity School, 1990), 6.
[7] Rempel, 13.
[8] InterAct Ministries, *Lazy Mountain Consultation Team Meeting*, 5 August 2013.
[9] Tom Steffen, *The Facilitator Era: Beyond Pioneer Church Multiplication* (Eugene: Wipf & Stock, 2011). 32.

Commission themselves.[10] Western missionaries should instead take the role of "facilitators," using their experience, training, and resources to empower indigenous Kingdom workers.[11] Based on the strategic consultations recounted above, Steffen's argument is directly applicable to the Inuit church. It is past time for Western pastors and missionaries to move out of the "pioneer" role and to facilitate the development of Inuit leaders.

Shane Mikeska describes an approach to discipleship that he labels "Life-on-Life Disciple-making" (LLDM), which is particularly relevant to this task in Alaska. Though Mikeska applies this in the context of evangelism among British secularists, its core relationally-driven principles are directly relevant to the question of leadership development among the Inuit. Contrasting his approach against what he calls "programmatic" discipleship curricula, which focus on outcome-based acquisition of knowledge and skills, Mikeska defines LLDM simply as "the combination of living life with the people around you and teaching them to know and obey the teachings of Jesus."[12] For Mikeska, discipleship is a fundamentally relational process, rooted in the "vertical" relationship between the disciple and God, and the "horizontal" relationship between fellow disciples. He summarizes,

> Relationships are the key to true disciple-making. If you don't have a relationship with someone how can you expect him or her to open up to you, to be held accountable, or to learn from one another? If a relationship exists then people can see our strengths and weaknesses, our failures and successes, and our growth and wisdom. Christians are all on a journey to continually allow God to transform us and make us more like Christ. We don't just one day arrive at being a super Christian and having it all figured out.[13]

This is just as true in an Inuit village as in the post-secular British city. The importance of relational discipleship in the present study will become clear with the discussion of relational logic later in this chapter. In this book, we adopt and adapt Mikeska's model of LLDM to the task of ministry leadership development in Inuit contexts.

To this end, two dissertations have been written on the topic of indigenous ministry leadership development among Northern peoples. Though neither focuses specifically on Inuit culture, both are helpful in illuminating the question at hand. In 1990, Gary Ridley's dissertation sought to contextualize

---

[10] Steffen, *The Facilitator Era*, 26.
[11] Steffen, *The Facilitator Era*, 73.
[12] Shane Mikeska, *Engaging the Secular World through Life-on-Life Disciple-making in the British Context* (DIS product, Western Seminary, 2017), 6.
[13] Mikeska, 150.

biblical leadership principles with leadership patterns indigenous to Alaska Natives. Ridley observed cultural leadership patterns in all four of the major groupings of Native peoples (including the Inuit), and compared these with biblical leadership principles. The primary cultural values pertaining to leadership in Inuit culture that emerged through Ridley's ethnography were informality, age/experience, knowledge, and character.[14] The result of his study was a paradigm for biblical leadership principles expressed in the Alaska Native context:

Alaska Native church leaders will:

1. Generally be at least thirty-five years old before they enter the pastoral role. (In some situations they may need to be older. The age of entering leadership roles is decreasing as the importance of higher education is increasing.)
2. Respect the wisdom of the elders.
3. Demonstrate leadership ability informally before taking a major leadership role.
4. Have a healthy self-image.
5. Appreciate their cultural heritage.
6. Recognize the process of acculturation and look to Scripture for guidance.
7. Model biblical teaching in the home and community.
8. Increasingly pursue Bible college and seminary education.
9. Lead informally and keep form appropriate to the needs of the congregation.
10. Influence their people to express godliness in their culture.
11. Be bivocational in the villages.
12. Submit to the authority of the Bible in all matters.[15]

Ridley's contextualized leadership paradigm remains quite helpful today. The cultural values on which it stands have not disappeared.

Ridley's dissertation closes with a proposal for how this paradigm could be implemented at Alaska Bible College to develop stronger indigenous leadership. Ridley was serving as president of this institution at the time, so it provided a natural avenue to apply his paradigm. His research had revealed the trend of increasing college education among young Alaska Natives and its importance for leadership roles in emerging Alaska Native corporations.[16] Ridley predicted this trend to continue and to carry over from state universities to the Bible

---

[14] Ridley, 61-66.
[15] Ridley, 103-104.
[16] Ridley, 84.

college. The Bible college, it seemed, would be the ideal place to develop leaders for the indigenous church in the 21st century.

Ridley's proposal for Alaska Bible College focused primarily on adapting the content of its Western curriculum for Native learners. Specifically, he sought to retool the existing "Leadership" course to address traditional leadership values.[17] The remainder of the curriculum focusing on biblical, theological, and ministry-related subject matter would remain relatively unchanged. Beyond this curricular adaptation, Ridley also offered several practical suggestions to make the Bible college a more welcoming environment for Alaska Native students.[18]

Thirty years later, it is clear that Ridley rightly predicted the rising importance of college education to job opportunities and future leadership roles among young Alaska Natives. Today more than ever, Alaska Native youth recognize the importance of college education to finding careers in the state's urban centers and, increasingly, their own local regions. Sadly, this trend has not translated to higher Native enrollment in the Bible college. So Ridley's contextualized paradigm remains quite culturally valid, but the vision of implementing it through the traditional Bible college environment has proven unsuccessful. The Inuit church must look to alternative models for indigenous leadership development.

The second dissertation on the topic of leadership development among Alaska Natives was written by Barry Rempel in 2014. Unlike Ridley, Rempel focused on one particular Alaska Native tribe, the Ahtna of the Copper River Valley. His purpose was "to discover perspectives and practices already embedded in the Ahtna culture that could serve as the foundation for a biblically sound and culturally relevant leadership development model."[19] Rempel took a narrower view of leadership development than Ridley, focusing specifically on "spiritual and cultural identity being fundamental components of leadership."[20] Spiritual and cultural identity were both evidenced in Ridley's paradigm, but Ridley also heavily emphasized the need for an understanding of the Bible, which is absent from Rempel's study.

Rempel's research provided key insight to the question of leadership development among the Ahtna people. Specifically, he found that five themes must inform the process:

> (1) a cultural perspective on leadership, (2) the importance of a well-developed cultural identity, (3) enhancing the role of women in leadership,

---

[17] Ridley, 104-106.
[18] Ridley, 106-108.
[19] Rempel, 2.
[20] Rempel, 5.

(4) a response to cataclysmic experiences, and (5) the pivotal place of mentoring in the leadership development process.[21]

It is noteworthy that all of these themes, with the exception of #3 (enhancing the role of women), echo similar points in the paradigm proposed by Gary Ridley. Since Rempel focused on general leadership principles that would apply to any context, issues unique to church leadership (in particular, understanding of Scripture) were not explored. It is also notable that both missionaries emphasize the importance of identity in the leadership development process.

Rempel's research demonstrates the importance of allowing local cultural values to inform the leadership development process. Rather than trying to incorporate the Ahtna into the Western leadership development model at Alaska Bible College, Rempel works towards a truly indigenous approach. The themes that he identifies in Ahtna culture could be incorporated into a distinctly Ahtna model for leadership development. Unfortunately, Rempel stops short of doing this himself, since his purpose was to discover the themes rather than to apply them.

Ridley and Rempel both demonstrate the process of identifying cultural themes pertinent to leadership development from a body of research data. Rempel's data was generated through action research, and Ridley gathered his through a combination of ethnography and archival work. Our approach in this book follows that of Ridley and Rempel by identifying cultural themes that impact the leadership development process in Inuit communities across the Arctic, and carries that research one step further by applying these themes to propose an alternative to the Western model of leadership development.

Worldview Studies

Paul Hiebert provides the theoretical foundation for this book in his 2008 volume, *Transforming Worldviews*. In this far-reaching treatment of the subject, Hiebert provides a helpful framework for worldview analysis that emphasizes how worldviews change over time. His extensive discussion of what he terms the "Modern Worldview" is particularly insightful for the present effort to critique the traditional Western approach of theological education and leadership training, which is a product of the modern worldview. Growing out of the epistemological traditions of empiricism and scientific positivism, the Western academy emphasizes propositional communication and analytical logic. Hiebert elaborates,

> In modernity the gospel increasingly was defined in terms of abstract doctrinal truths, not everyday living. The result was the development of

---
[21] Rempel, 112-113.

systematic theology as a kind of science based on positivist presuppositions, a grand unified theory that explained everything. Truth was to be determined by rational argument and encoded in propositional statements linked by reason. This work of experts assumed that human rationality is based on universal, transcultural, and transhistorical laws of thought. Moreover, to be objective, truth had to be separated from affectivity and morality.[22]

Hiebert demonstrates how this thought pattern, so intrinsically ingrained in traditional approaches to theological education, excludes equally valid systems of thought and expression that characterize non-modernist worldviews to varying degrees.[23] Two such systems that are particularly relevant to the study at hand are relational logic and narrative logic.

Hiebert acknowledged the relational orientation of many non-Western thought patterns when he argued, "If our being in community is the essence of our identity, we must regard relational sets as of greater importance than intrinsic sets. It also calls for thinking in terms of relational rather than abstract analytical logic."[24] Although he nudged Western missionaries in this direction, the relational aspect remained relatively undeveloped in the critical realist paradigm that he proposed as an answer to modernism. To address this shortcoming, Dr. Wan proposed the paradigm of "Relational Realism." In relational realism, we seek to shift the center of discourse from the individual to the community and to acknowledge relational logic over and above (or at least in addition to) analytical logic. In short, "Human understanding is best comprehended and experienced in relational networks."[25] Applied to the question of leadership development, relational logic provides a key toolkit that can be particularly valuable in the context of collectivistic worldviews.

The paradigm of relational realism has been received with mixed results. In his 2007 follow-up to his initial proposal, Dr. Wan observed,

> readers who are not preconditioned by the traditional theological orientation of the West may find "relational paradigm" self-evident. Others, who are so entrenched theologically in Western tradition may immediately

---

[22] Hiebert, *Transforming Worldviews*, 195.
[23] These "non-modernist" worldviews would include not only the worldviews of non-Western cultures such as the Inuit, but also the postmodern and "post-postmodern" or "glocal" worldviews that Hiebert identifies as later developments in Western thought.
[24] Hiebert, *Transforming Worldviews*, 288.
[25] Wan, "Relational Realism," 1.

dismiss "relational paradigm" to be a corruption by existentialism, postmodernism and neo-orthodoxy.[26]

Indeed, relational realism can be difficult for those accustomed to thinking in systematic propositions and analytical logic to evaluate. It is for these same reasons that critical realism is more readily accepted by Westerners as an improvement over positivism, idealism, and instrumentalism.

The critical realist looks at human knowledge as a "map" corresponding to reality. A map provides a synchronic view of reality—a snapshot in time. This is consistent with Hiebert's early discussion of signs, which emphasized "words, gestures, sounds, and other signfiers."[27] At this point in his thinking at least, Hiebert understood signs as primarily synchronic and propositional in nature. (Though he would not argue that language changes over time, his emphasis on the use of a particular word at a specific point in time is a synchronic discussion.) The relational realist, on the other hand, views knowledge through a constantly-developing network of relationships that shapes how reality is understood. Relationships are inherently diachronic in nature. They begin, develop, ebb, flow, and sometimes end. In order for dialog or integration to occur between the two paradigms, a diachronic understanding of semiotics is needed. This is provided by the concept of story, as recently explored by Michael Matthews and Tom Steffen—missiologists working in the emerging field of orality.

Matthews defines "story" as "an interpreted account of a series of related events that entail character, setting and plot."[28] He goes on to explore how these interpreted accounts are foundational to human understanding of reality. Every person, every group, every nation has a story that explains its identity and its place in the world. "Story is interpretive—the major factor in how we determine meaning. And story is formative—the foundation and fountain of every culture's core assumptions regarding reality."[29]

According to this definition, story can easily be understood as another category of Peircean "sign," linking mental images to the real world. As Steffen observes, "Story helps conceptualize experience, interpret reality, provide identity, and offer a community of insiders. It does this at least in part because story serves both as a mirror (reflects back) and as a window (see through)."[30] Matthews goes as far as to say, "A story is a slice of reality, in terms of time and

---

[26] Enoch Wan, "Relational Theology and Relational Missiology," *EMS Occasional Bulletin*, vol. 21, no. 1 (Fall 2007), 1-8, 2.
[27] Hiebert, *Missiological Implications*, 71.
[28] Michael Matthews, *A Novel Approach: The Significance of Story in Interpreting Reality* (Victoria: Tellwell, 2017). 88.
[29] Matthews, 83.
[30] Steffen, *Worldview-based Storying*, 142.

space, as perceived, interpreted, and narrated by someone."[31] Just like individual words and propositions (as emphasized by Hiebert), stories provide a sort of map or grid through which humans understand truth and reality.

Stories, however, are markedly different than individual words and concepts in that they provide a diachronic view of reality rather than merely synchronic. The word "tree" will generally conjure mental images of some sort of large, woody plant. However, let me tell you a *story* that begins with a tree in a garden, climaxes with a tree on a hill faraway, and ends with a tree in a beautiful city next to a river flowing from a throne. N.T. Wright claims that because of this diachronic perspective, "Narrative is the most characteristic expression of worldview, going deeper than the isolated observation or fragmented remark."[32] The signs preferred by Western logic, including critical realism as Hiebert initially described it, are basically propositional in nature. Westerners think systematically and often default to words, statements, and bullet points. Narrative provides an alternate but equally valid form of expression.

We propose that they provide the diachronic signs that are needed to conceptualize our relational networks. Characters are intrinsic to story. Every story revolves around relationship. Most involve human-to-human relationships of some sort, but some also focus on other relationships within the created order. Even those that revolve purely around some sort of "internal" conflict explore the relationship (or lack thereof) between a human being and the Triune God. Without relationship, there is no story. Therefore, Matthews argues,

> Story is inherently Trinitarian. Before everything other than the God of the Scriptures existed there were characters (the Trinity), there was setting (the Trinity), and there was plot (the Trinity). *Story consists of character, setting, and plot.* That is a definition of story: pre-creation, pared down to bare bones. It zeros in on the structure and fundamental elements of story. Story did not come upon the scene with the dawn of Genesis 1:1; its essence exists eternally within the environment of the Trinity.[33]

Human stories, like all other aspects of reality, find their source in the Triune God, Stories are not relationships. Rather, stories are dynamic, diachronic signs that are generated by relationships to reflect and communicate reality. Relationships inevitably produce stories, and just as all relationships can be diagrammed across time and space, so all stories can find their place in the grand metanarrative—the greatest story. These stories, in turn, allow humans

---

[31] Matthews, 88.
[32] N.T. Wright, *The New Testament and the People of God* (Minneapolis: Fortress, 1992). 123.
[33] Matthews, 85.

to understand and reflect on reality not as an individualistic cognitive exercise, but rather as relational agents living and interacting in community within the created order and with the Triune Creator.

Having established a theoretical framework that allows for dialog between analytical, relational, and narrative forms of logic, attention now turns to the ramifications of relational and narrative logic in the question of ministry leadership development. Several important areas of sociological and missiological theory have particular bearing on this discussion: education, leadership, social control, and orality.

Educational Theory

Education is one specific area of culture and worldview in which relational logic has important implications. Though Western schools were only established among the Inuit within the last 300 years, education in and of itself is of course not a new phenomenon. The Inuit have been teaching their children to survive and to thrive in this environment for thousands of years using tried and true methods. Article 14.1 of the UN Declaration on the Rights of Indigenous Peoples argues that these methods must inform today's educational efforts: "Indigenous peoples have the right to establish and control their educational systems and institutions providing education in their own languages, in a manner appropriate to their cultural methods of teaching and learning."[34]

Ministry leadership development is a fundamentally educational process according to Jesus' emphasis on "teaching" in Matthew 28:20. Though discipleship occurs at all ages, our concern in this book is the discipleship of adults for leadership roles in the church. So, how can adult Inuit believers learn the necessary skills, knowledge, and behavior for leadership in the church? The concern here is not as much on the content, but rather the process of the training. Each church or denomination will have its own training priorities, including some combination of scriptural knowledge, theological and exegetical skills, character formation, and ministry practice. Regardless of *what* is taught, appropriate cultural forms and practices must be used in the process.

Not all pedagogical principles transfer directly to andragogy. The education of children is primarily informational in nature—the basics of reading, writing, and arithmetic, for example—and this is the focus of most research on Inuit education. Adult education, and Christian discipleship in particular, is more transformative in nature. The goal is not only to relay new information, but to transform the character of the student by encouraging critical reflection and

---

[34] United Nations, General Assembly, *United Nations Declaration on the Rights of Indigenous Peoples*, A/61/L.67 (7 September 2007). 6.

constructive discourse.³⁵ In Christian contexts, this occurs primarily through relationship with God and the faith community, as Dr. Wan and Mark Hedinger have argued in an earlier volume that provides the relational framework for Christian transformative learning that is applied in this study:

> Transformative learning is a matter of allowing the spirit of truth to transform the heart, as well as the mind through relationship with God vertically and fellow Christians within the body of Christ horizontally… In contrast to secular education focusing primarily on learning knowledge, information, and skills, relational Christian adult education must focus on "being" and "doing," individually and collectively including assumptions and beliefs that drive their perspectives (or worldviews) leading to a new reality in Christ and new humanity in the Church.³⁶

Leadership Theory

Leadership is a second cultural domain in which the application of relational logic can inform the development of ministry leaders among the Inuit. The framework of "Relational Leadership Theory" (RLT), proposed by Mary Uhl-Bien, provides the necessary theoretical framework for the present study:

> Contrary to other studies of leadership, which have focused primarily on the study of leadership effectiveness, Relational Leadership Theory focuses on the relational processes by which leadership is produced and enabled. It does not define leadership as holding a managerial position, nor does it use the terms manager and leader interchangeably. It sees leadership as able to occur in any direction; in some variations, it may result in the breakdown of the distinction between who is leading and who is following, instead reflecting a mutual influence process.³⁷

Rather than defining leadership according to predetermined roles, Uhl-Bien defines leadership as "a *social influence process* through which emergent coordination (e.g., evolving social order) and change (e.g., new values, attitudes, approaches, behaviors, ideologies, etc.) are constructed and produced."³⁸ Leadership development from the perspective of RLT, then, is not a matter of starting with a job description and "working backwards" through a series of courses and experiences to produce a person who fits the criteria. Rather, it is a

---

³⁵ Jack Mezirow, "Learning to Think Like an Adult: Core Concepts of Transformation Theory," in *Learning as Transformation: Critical Perspectives on a Theory in Progress* (San Francisco: Jossey-Bass, 2000). 7-8
³⁶ Enoch Wan & Mark Hedinger, *Relational Missionary Training* (Skyforest: Urban Loft, 2017). 120-121.
³⁷ Mary Uhl-Bien, "Relational Leadership Theory: Exploring the Social Processes of Leadership and Organizing," *Leadership Quarterly*, vol. 17 (2006), 654-676, 667.
³⁸ Uhl-Bien, 668. Emphasis mine.

matter of identifying how leadership emerges through existing relationships within the community. Indeed, "the focus of investigation in Relational Leadership Theory would be on how relational interactions contribute to the generation and emergence of social order."[39]

Social Control Theory

Another area of worldview that is important to ministry leadership development is social control. This area too has important relational aspects. Social control describes the various methods that people of a given society use to mediate relationships and govern behavior. Social control incentivizes certain behaviors deemed desirable by the community and corrects behaviors that are undesirable. Anthropologists identify three primary avenues of social control in cultures worldwide: "gossip, scandal, and ridicule" (i.e., "Shame/Honor"), fear of "supernatural sanctions" (i.e., "Fear/Power"), and "legal punishment" (i.e., "Guilt/Innocence").[40] In 2000, Roland Muller applied this theory of social control to the question of intercultural ministry, demonstrating how the dynamics of Guilt/Innocence, Shame/Honor, and Fear/Power can be understood both in terms of their effects on human-to-human relationships as well as human-to-divine.[41] Jayson Georges elaborates on these dynamics as follows:

> (1) guilt-innocence cultures are individualistic societies (mostly Western), where people who break the laws are guilty and seek justice or forgiveness to rectify a wrong, (2) shame-honor cultures describes collectivistic cultures (common in the East), where people shamed for fulfilling group expectations seek to restore their honor before the community, and (3) fear-power cultures refers to animistic contexts (typically tribal or African), where people afraid of evil and harm pursue power over the spirit world through magical rituals.[42]

Though Muller was originally focused primarily on how these dynamics should influence the presentation of the gospel message between cultures, Georges, along with Mark Baker, has called attention to how these issues shape relationships within the Christian community: "by operating according to the logic and values of our default culture, we have often unknowingly sown hurt and alienation in honor-shame contexts."[43] Since Western patterns of

---

[39] Uhl-Bien, 670.
[40] Garrick Bailey & James Peoples, *Introduction to Cultural Anthropology* (Belmont: Wadsworth, 1999), 189.
[41] Roland Muller, *Honor & Shame: Unlocking the Door* (Bloomington: Xlibris, 2000), 18-19.
[42] Jayson Georges, *The 3D Gospel* (N.p.: Time, 2014), 11.
[43] Jayson Georges & Mark D. Baker, *Ministering in Honor-Shame Cultures* (Downers Grove: InterVarsity, 2016), 134.

leadership development are so heavily steeped in Guilt/Innocence orientation, a relational approach must give careful consideration to how the Shame/Honor orientation should inform the process of leadership development in collectivistic societies.

Orality Theory

The final major theoretical framework with significant bearing on the present study is orality. As demonstrated earlier, orality and relationship go hand-in-hand, and again, Hiebert's treatment provides the "seedbed" for this understanding:

> Oral communication is highly relational. It takes place in specific contexts, is spoken to a particular audience or person, and focuses on particular messages. It communicates paramessages, such as feelings and moral judgments, through tone of voice, gesture, facial expressions, and standing distances. It requires listening and responding as well as remembering. It invites moral judgment and response.[44]

Tom Steffen explores the topic of orality in great detail, providing a helpful comparison between the "narrative logic" of oral societies and the analytical (or "propositional") logic favored in the traditional seminary environment:

> For those unfamiliar with narrative logic, story seems messy, full of ambiguity, subjective, borderless, inconsistent, tentative, contradictory, complex, unfinished, unresolved, open to multiple meanings. That is often because researchers rely on propositional logic to interpret story in search of a single definitive answer (which may carry some Enlightenment baggage). Narrative logic, however, works differently and has different goals.[45]

Story, then, is an essential principle that will have key bearing on a relational approach to leadership development.

Steffen proposes the idea of "worldview-based storying" to guide practitioners in orality-based ministry. In his historical survey of orality-based methods to date, he observes that ministries have tended to assume that simply telling scriptural stories will ensure the comprehension of the gospel message across cultures. He points out that such a presupposition implicitly assumes that all cultures interpret stories in the same way.[46] Moreover, the storyteller's natural inclination is to tell stories from their own cultural perspective, making certain points of emphasis and ignoring others altogether (for example, most

---

[44] Hiebert, *Transforming Worldviews*, 116.
[45] Steffen, *Worldview-based Storying*, 135.
[46] Steffen, *Worldview-based Storying*, 105.

Western curricula emphasize a heavy guilt/innocence framework and ignore shame/honor, fear/power, and pollution/purity orientations).[47] Even the selection of which stories to tell is culturally-informed. To remedy this bias, Steffen calls cross-cultural storytellers to perform a careful study of local worldviews and to shape their curricula accordingly. By identifying how local cultures interpret the world through their own "common," "anchor," and "master" stories (along with associated symbols and rituals), cross-cultural storytellers will be better able to transpose the master story of Scripture onto that worldview, leading to genuine and meaningful change.[48]

Steffen's colleague Michael Matthews provides a comprehensive framework for this worldview-based approach to orality in *A Novel Approach*. Matthews argues that as relational beings, story is intrinsic to humans' understanding and experience of reality:

> We all interpret based upon our incarnation and participation in some grand story. Despite the parental curse of Adam on all, followers of Christ, by the grace of God, have the privilege of being able to exegete reality correctly, at least to some degree, here on Earth. They do not comprehend completely, but they comprehend sufficiently. They have a greater understanding, appreciation, and assistance regarding what is real which has been derived from living in fellowship with the Trinity and with the Spirit-led historic community of Christ-followers in this earthly portion of the ultimate grand story.[49]

Of course, not all stories carry equal weight in a person's understanding of reality. Both Matthews and Steffen offer categories that demonstrate how stories intersect and interrelate in their depiction of reality. Matthews uses the terms "episode," "key story," and "grand story,"[50] which are analogous to the "common story," "anchor story," and "master story" described by Steffen.[51] To these categories, Matthews adds a fourth, the "greatest story," which is a metanarrative encapsulating all other stories—God's dealings within the Trinity and with creation from eternity to eternity. Matthews provides a detailed process outlining how to evaluate a culture's oral traditions to identify the key stories and grand stories, with the ultimate goal of weaving them into the greatest story. In this way, every individual in every culture can trace his or her own story back to the ultimate metanarrative of God's dealings from eternity to eternity.

---

[47] Steffen, *Worldview-based Storying*, 109.
[48] Steffen, *Worldview-based Storying*, 200-201.
[49] Matthews, 98.
[50] Matthews, 89.
[51] Steffen, *Worldview-based Storying*, 127.

Orality theory intersects with the theme of leadership development on two levels. First, in terms of pedagogy, traditional seminary curricula tend to rely heavily on literacy (reading and writing) to the exclusion of orally based learning. This can present a significant challenge to oral-preference learners. To this end, the ethnographic research at hand identifies whether and how orality should be featured in Inuit education over and above literacy. Second, in terms of curricular design, the "worldview-based storytelling approach" outlined by Steffen and Matthews informs goals for biblical literacy in Inuit church leaders. In other words, by researching the worldview and oral traditions of the Inuit, a glocalized biblical curriculum or story sequence can be developed that answers the questions and addresses the issues raised in their own key and grand stories by weaving in the metanarrative of Scripture.

The "Glocal" Approach

This book employs a form of ethnographic research known as "ethnology" to develop a "glocal" model of leadership development that can be adapted for use in Inuit communities across the Arctic. Whereas traditional ethnography emphasizes study of one particular community or ethnic group through participant observation and other forms of fieldwork, ethnology compares ethnographic data from several different communities or groups to identify patterns, shared values, and common themes. R. Burke Johnson and Larry Christensen provide a helpful definition and illustration of this research method:

> It involves conducting or comparing a series of separate ethnographic studies of the same or different cultural groups to uncover general patterns and rules of social behavior. For example, ethnology might involve the comparison of family practices or educational practices in several different cultures. The ethnologist would look for similarities and differences among the groups.[52]

Isabelle Fleming provides further elaboration on the nature of ethnology:

> Ethnology is highly theory driven, using a comparative approach with the writings of ethnographers to search for commonalities that may underlie all cultures or human behaviors. In addition, ethnology takes a broad view, comparing cultures or looking at the deep history of a culture in order to explain why and how it functions as it does.[53]

---

[52] R. Burke Johnson & Larry Christensen, *Educational Research: Quantitative, Qualitative, and Mixed Approaches*, 6th ed. (Los Angeles: Sage, 2017).
[53] Isabelle M. Flemming, "Ethnography and Ethnology," in *21st Century Anthropology: A Reference Handbook*, vol. 1 (Los Angeles: Sage, 2010) 153-161. 153.

Though he does not use the term "ethnology," Gary Ridley employed this approach in his dissertation on leadership development in Alaska Native cultures. His discussion of research methodology is helpful to consider here:

> The ethnographic research in this project focuses primarily on the ethnographic literature on Alaska Natives. Leadership patterns constitute the area of concern in this regard. Extensive research has been carried out in order to locate material on traditional patterns of leadership among the Alaskan Natives. The writer first surveyed the Ethnographic literature for monographs and articles on Native leadership. This was followed by an examination of general Ethnographies looking for discussion on social organization, political organization and ranking. The Ethnographic literature was then surveyed for monographs and articles on cultural and social change among the Alaska Natives. The sources uncovered became the basis for the study of Native leadership patterns.[54]

This approach allowed Ridley to develop what might be anachronistically labeled a "glocal" profile of an Alaska Native leader. In this book, we employ the same methodological approach, but focus on the circumpolar Inuit people groups rather than the indigenous peoples of Alaska that were the focus of Ridley's study. The Inuit people have hosted many English language ethnographic researchers, and this wealth of literature provides ample data for an ethnological profile of leadership development across the Inuit arctic.

The "glocal" approach was introduced by Tom Steffen as part of his discussion of the Western church's shift from a pioneer to facilitator role, as discussed earlier. He provides a helpful comparison that defines the glocal approach in comparison to two others:

> There are basically three models available: global, glocal, and local. Global narrative evangelism models are imported; it's one curriculum fits all, one for all the world. Glocal narrative evangelism models assume that one curriculum fits some. Designers develop several generic models that target a wide, but specific, audience—say Buddhists, Muslims, Hindus, animists, secularists, atheists. The last, local narrative evangelism models, refers to curricula designed specifically for a particular audience, like what we did for our people group. It's one fits one. So we have one for all, one for some, and one for one.[55]

Traditionally, theological education and leadership development have been carried out through a global model. The assumption has been that what works for the West will work for the rest. The Western education system that

---

[54] Ridley, 10.
[55] Steffen, *Facilitator Era*, 143.

developed in Europe as a product of the Industrial Revolution has been exported and implemented around the world, and most seminaries and Bible colleges tend to offer variations on the same basic core curriculum, regardless of context. While this approach is cost effective, Steffen argues that it introduces unnecessary noise into the educational process that reduces its effectiveness among specific local audiences: "Transferred curricula should have no part in the storyteller's story sets. Why? Because 'Comprehended stories are contextualized stories.'"[56] While a specific local curricular model for every people group would be ideal, Steffen points out that this approach is not always the best stewardship of time and resources.[57] Considering the cultural similarities and shared experiences of Inuit people groups across the Arctic, as well as the small population sizes of individual communities, a glocal approach offers a culturally-relevant training model that can be applied in a wide swath of Inuit communities.

Summary

The theoretical background for our study of Inuit leadership development is now in place. We have established the importance of leadership development to the church's missiological task, and observed that this step of the task remains unfinished in the Inuit church as a whole. Through the lens of a relational worldview, we have identified four major areas of anthropological theory that impact this task: education, leadership, social control, and orality. Lastly, we have explained the "glocal" scope of our work and established the relevance this approach. With these pieces in place, our attention turns to the methodological context of the book.

---

[56] Steffen, *Worldview-based Storying*, 204-205.
[57] Steffen, *Facilitator Era*, 143.

Chapter 3
Overview of Leadership Development Programs

Introduction

Having established the theoretical context for our discussion of Inuit ministry leadership development, our attention now turns to the methodological context—the practical realities of day-to-day ministry in the Arctic. In this chapter, you will meet the key characters—both historic and contemporary—who are involved in the development of Inuit church leaders. Through their experiences and stories—both successes and failures—a portrait of effective leadership development will begin to emerge. This survey is organized by country according to the historical development of Christianity in Inuit regions. Within each country, major Evangelical ministries are discussed roughly according to the order in which they began to serve the Inuit. Through this survey, we will begin to identify some key factors that contribute to successful leadership development in Inuit contexts.

Greenland

Christianity was introduced to the southwestern coast of Greenland in the eleventh century by Norse settlers from Iceland led by Erik the Red.[58] At this time, the area was largely uninhabited, as the Greenlandic (Kalaallit) Inuit, known as the *skræling* to the Norse, were only just migrating across Baffin Bay from Canada in the far north. The Norse established a Catholic diocese in southern Greenland that endured until approximately 1500. The reasons for the settlement's demise are not clear, but it is likely that an extended cooling in global climate patterns during this time decimated the agricultural lifestyle of the Norse and simultaneously allowed the Inuit to extend their subsistence-based culture further south, displacing and perhaps assimilating the Norse settlements.[59] At any rate, the Catholic presence in Greenland was a distinctly European phenomenon, and there was no documented effort to evangelize the Inuit to the north.

In 1721, the Norwegian missionary Hans Egede was dispatched to Greenland by the King of Denmark, which claimed Greenland as a colony.[60]

---

[58] Stephen Neill, *A History of Christian Missions*, 2nd ed. (London: Penguin, 1986), 92.
[59] Frank Darnel & Anton Hoëm, *Taken to Extremes: Education in the Far North* (Oslo: Scandinavian University, 1996. 111.
[60] Neill, 200.

Egede's goal was to make contact with the lost Catholic settlements, which had not been heard from for 200 years, and to convert them to the state's new Lutheran faith.[61] Though the Norse colony was nowhere to be found, Egede found an audience for the Gospel message in the Inuit who now populated the coastline of southwest Greenland—albeit not without a significant linguistic barrier.[62] Egede was soon joined by a group of Moravian missionaries in led by Christian David in 1733, who had heard that the Lutheran effort was likely to be abandoned.[63] Though the rumors proved untrue, the Moravians remained and worked alongside Egede and the Lutherans until 1900, though not always without a spirit of competition.

A hallmark of both the Moravian and Lutheran missionary efforts was to minister in the indigenous Inuit language of Kalaallisut.[64] To support this growing indigenous movement, two schools were established for the training of Greenlandic teachers and clergy in 1847.[65] Instruction was provided in both Greenlandic and Danish, but the curricular approach was distinctly European—an extension of the system already in use in Denmark.[66] Though the school in Ilullissat since closed, the one in Nuuk remains to this day, having been incorporated into Ilisimatusarfik, or the University of Greenland, in 2008.[67]

Though the schools produced Greenlandic pastors for the Lutheran church over the years, and the majority of the indigenous population nominally identifies with the state-sponsored Lutheran Church of Greenland (which is itself a diocese of the Church of Denmark), there exist few Evangelical believers among the Greenlandic Inuit today. Like most of the mainline churches of Europe and North America, the Church of Denmark was heavily influenced by the rise of theological liberalism in the early twentieth century. Most Greenlandic Inuit today would claim Christianity as their religion but could not explain the gospel or affirm the historic tenets of the Christian faith. The school that provided many early Greenlandic pastors now emphasizes business and social sciences, with no theological emphasis evident in its course listings.[68]

A predominant contemporary Evangelical presence in Greenland is found in the Plymouth Brethren assemblies established by the Faroese. William Gibson Sloan introduced a strong Brethren presence in the Faroe Islands (which are

---

[61] Ruth Tucker, *From Jerusalem to Irian Jaya: A Biographical History of Christian Missions* (Grand Rapids: Zondervan, 1983). 75.
[62] Neill, 200-201.
[63] Neill, 202.
[64] Darnel & Hoëm, 113.
[65] Darnel & Hoëm, 116.
[66] Darnel & Hoëm, 117.
[67] Darnel & Hoëm, 116.
[68] "Programmes and Courses," *Ilisimatusarfik*, https://uk.uni.gl/international/guest-students-at-ilisimatusarfik/programmes-and-courses.aspx (Accessed 26 August 2020).

also a territory of Denmark) in the late 1800s.[69] Faroese fishermen and sailors living in Greenland have since established a small Evangelical presence in the country. Though services are conducted in Danish, Inuit are welcome to attend, and some have come to faith. I (John) have fond memories of attending a weeklong evangelistic summer camp alongside many Inuit children that was sponsored by the Brethren assembly in Nuuk in 1992.

Firm Foundations (Ethnos360)

It was one of the Inuit converts from the Brethren assembly who approached New Tribes Mission (now Ethnos360) in the mid-1980s, inviting the organization to send a church planting team to Greenland to establish a truly indigenous gospel witness among the Inuit. Founded in 1942, New Tribes Mission was established to plant self-governing, self-sustaining, and self-propagating indigenous churches in areas with no contemporary gospel witness:

> New Tribes Mission's efforts shall be directed toward those fields where no other missionary effort is being made and where no witness of the gospel has yet reached. Self-propagation of the native churches shall be encouraged. Every means at our disposal shall be employed to bring the churches to a self-sustaining basis. Native workers shall be encouraged and trained to become effective Christian leaders, and the responsibility of the work shall be passed on to them as quickly as possible.[70]

Though historically working in remote tropical locations, mission administrators purportedly had no answer when asked by the Inuit believer, "Does New Tribes Mission work only where it is hot?"—an anecdote that I frequently heard my father share with supporting churches during our family's deputation process.

My father, Gary Ferch, was a member of the team sent to survey the country for a potential church planting effort, and in 1988 my family moved to the Inuit village of Paamiut. He served as team leader for the next four years. My parents' ministry report in the organizational newsletter *Brown Gold* summarizes the early days of the effort:

> On our survey trip to Northern Greenland, we became settled in our thinking about two things of the Uummannaq district. First, it is one of the most extremely majestic places in the world. And secondly, no evangelical witness exists among these hearty folk, ranking it high priority for evangelism and church planting... The Greenlandic language study is the center of our

---

[69] Fred Kelling, *Fisherman of Faroe: William Gibson Sloan* (Gota: Leirkerid, 1993).
[70] Rosie Cochran, *Founded: The Heritage of Ethnos360* (Sanford: Ethnos360, 2017). 37-38.

activity. Here is a sample: *Iluamik oqalussinnanngilanga* which means, "I can't speak it right yet." One young Greenlandic couple, Mikael and Naja, have helped us so much in learning language and their way of life. We have enjoyed some good times with them, hunting and fishing and eating whale meat and *matik* (blubber).[71]

After nearly five years of ministry, Danish immigration policy prevented my parents from serving in Greenland any longer. After their departure, the ministry continued through Scandinavian missionaries who were not subject to the same immigration restrictions. The team carried on over the years, committed to Ethnos360's strategy of achieving fluency in the indigenous language, followed by an in-depth chronological study of the Bible known as "Firm Foundations."

Steffen has provided a thorough overview and analysis of this approach, which in his view "launched the present-day evangelical Orality Movement… in January 1981."[72] The curriculum consists of nine volumes, the first of which introduces the philosophical and methodological foundations. The remaining volumes consist of a series of Bible lessons progressing in roughly chronological order from Genesis to Revelation.[73] Volume 2 ("Phase 1" of the curriculum) is evangelistic in its intent, tracing the gospel story (from a markedly "guilt-innocence" perspective) "from Creation to Christ."[74] Phases 2-4 are aimed towards discipleship of new believers, reviewing the stories from Creation to Christ from this perspective, and introducing the Acts and Epistles.[75] Phases 5-7 are aimed at mature believers, reviewing the entire counsel of Scripture to develop deep theological concepts.[76] The ultimate goal is that through this comprehensive and cumulative development of God's word, natural leaders in the host culture will receive sufficient biblical training to oversee the developing church.[77]

After nearly thirty years of ministry in Greenland with Ethnos360, Norwegian missionary Anne-Marit Skare has led small groups of Inuit through the first four phases of the Firm Foundations curriculum. She explained the process that she found effective: "I have been blessed with several good Bible students. I teach chronological through the Bible in small groups, at the

---

[71] Gary & Donna Ferch, "Greenland," *Brown Gold* (February 1990), 5.
[72] Steffen, *Worldview-based Storying*, 42.
[73] Steffen, *Worldview-based Storying*, 43.
[74] Trevor McIlwain, *Building on Firm Foundations: Guidelines for Evangelism & Teaching Believers*, Revised Edition (Sanford: New Tribes Mission, 2005). 80.
[75] McIlwain, 82-84.
[76] McIlwain, 85.
[77] McIlwain, 68.

moment two in each group. I find that very effective. Some of my Bible students have started to teach others also."[78]

Skare also provided a detailed description of how she presented the lessons:

> I always read the text in the Bible. This to underline that the Bible is God's Word, and the only place we find God's Word. The students also got the lesson with the main points, and additional Bible verses. We read together the lesson and all the Bible verses. Homework: repeat the lesson, read all the verses, and answer the questions. Next time we went through the questions.[79]

From this description, it is clear that she relied primarily on literacy skills (reading and writing) in her approach to teaching. That said, the small group approach allowed her to be flexible according to each student's needs:

> Some pick up the message very well. The teaching sessions were 1 ½ hour or more. Some were really clever and fast in their learning. But others were not able to concentrate for that amount of time, so I just had half a lesson with them, or as far as they managed. And some needed counselling before they were able to take in the Bible message. This because of their difficult childhood.[80]

Though Skare relocated from Greenland to Norway in 2018, the ministry of Ethnos360 continues under Filip & Ane Sivertsen and Oli & Anne-Sophie Tindalid—two younger ethnically-European families from Greenland who continue to teach through the Firm Foundations curriculum in small groups.[81] To date, no Greenlandic Inuit have completed the entire training to emerge as leaders for the church.

Greenlandic Free Church (Inuunerup Nutaap Oqaluffia)

More recently, the Free Church of Greenland, *Inuunerup Nutaap Oqaluffia* ("New Life Church"), reports local home groups in fourteen of Greenland's villages.[82] This organization has its roots in a conglomeration of Pentecostal outreaches including the Danish *missionshusene* ("missions houses"), the

---

[78] Anne-Marit Skare, "Information About Greenland," email to John Ferch, 15 October 2014.
[79] Anne-Marit Skare, "Inuit Ministry in Greenland," email to John Ferch, 7 September 2020.
[80] Skare, "Inuit Ministry in Greenland."
[81] "Standing Firm," *New Tribes Mission UK*, 21 February 2020, https://www.ntm.org.uk/news/standing-firm/ (Accessed 8 September 2020.)
[82] "The Greenlandic Free Churches," *Inuunerup Nutaap Oqaluffia*, https://ino.gl/kirker (Accessed 8 September 2020).

Apostolic Church, and the Assemblies of God.[83] Though little information is published regarding their leadership or training methods, correspondence with Katharina and Peter De Graaf, a Dutch missionary couple serving the INO congregation in Tasiilaq, provided some details:

> [T]here is no formal pastoral training in the INO churches. But most churches (all except the one here in Tasiilaq) are led by Inuit pastors. In Nuuk for example the church was taken over by a young Inuit about three years ago when the Danish missionary left after 30 years. There has been one on one discipling for about 2 years to prepare him for the job. And I think this is mostly how people grow into the role of a pastor here. They grow in their walk with the Lord and, where fit they are growing into church leadership.[84]

This suggests that the group has been successful in developing Inuit pastoral leadership by using non-formal, experientially-based, on-site discipleship methods. Elaborating on these methods, Katharina De Graaf clarified:

> We believe relationship is crucial to discipleship... we started a little Bible class to help the new believers grow in their faith. We have seen however that frontal teaching does not yield the change we long for. So last year we have made a shift to Bible story telling. That also gives the believers more overall Bible knowledge, as indeed that is an issue here.[85]

Comparing these two contemporary Evangelical efforts in Greenland, Ethnos360 emphasizes curricular content, while the INO churches emphasize practical ministry experience. Both have their shortcomings. Ethnos360 has not trained any Inuit pastors in over 30 years of ministry. INO has many Inuit pastors, but their biblical knowledge is an acknowledged weakness. It seems that an integration of the two approaches could be helpful.

Alaska

The gospel message first came to Alaska not from the Global West, but from the East. Russian fur traders, or *promyshlenniki*, braved what would later be known as the Bering Strait, following the prized sea otter population from island to island across the Aleutian chain that stretches from Siberia to Alaska. Under official charter from the Russian czar, the Danish explorer Vitus Bering led the first expedition to officially complete this voyage in 1741, charting the

---

[83] "Frikirke-fusion på vej i Grønland," *Kristeligt Dagblad*, 4 September 1999, https://www.kristeligt-dagblad.dk/kirke-tro/frikirke-fusion-p%C3%A5-vej-i-gr%C3%B8nland (Accessed 8 September 2020).
[84] Katharina de Graaf, "hjælp med forskning," email to John Ferch, 10 September 2020.
[85] Katharina de Graaf, "hjælp med forskning," email to John Ferch, 22 September 2020.

coastline and reporting his discovery back to the imperial capital. Bering's discovery provided Imperial Russia with a foothold in the New World and opened the door for scores of treasure hunters seeking to make a name for themselves off this new frontier. Though the Russian presence brought a limited degree of European influence to Inuit regions, Russia's economic interests lay primarily in the resource-rich regions to the south, inhabited by the Unangan, Sugpiaq, and Tlingit peoples.

The sale of "Russian America" to the United States with the Treaty of Cession in 1867 signaled great changes for the Church in Alaska. Though Russian political involvement ceased, the Orthodox Church was given specific protections under the treaty, and it continued to operate as the only notable Christian presence in the territory for nearly twenty years. Reeling from the aftermath of the Civil War, the federal government largely ignored its latest acquisition, leaving it primarily under military rule.[86] No federal court had jurisdiction, and few federal laws even applied to the region, leading to an escalation of violence as residents took matters into their own hands.[87] It was not until the passage of the Organic Act in 1884, twenty years after the transfer, that civil government was reestablished in the region.[88] The stage was set for the major American denominations to take up the mantle of missionary work in Alaska.

The primary proponent for the Organic Act was the Presbyterian minister Sheldon Jackson, who was the superintendent of Presbyterian Missions in the Territories. Jackson had taken keen interest in Alaska since 1877, when he received a letter from an army private stationed in Wrangell that highlighted the plight of the local Tlingit people:

> Since the advent of the traders and miners among them, lewdness and debauchery have held high carnival, and the decimation of their numbers is the result. If a school and mission were established at Wrangell there would, no doubt, be an Indian population of over 1000 souls located within reach of its benefits… Can you not, will you not, make it your business to build up and foster this mission to Alaska?[89]

Though he never personally resided in Alaska, Jackson answered this call and did indeed make it his business to establish Christian missionary outreach throughout the region. Jackson immediately began to lobby Congress to

---

[86] Claus M. Naske & Herman E. Slotnick, *Alaska: A History*, 3rd ed. (Norman: University of Oklahoma, 2011), 109.
[87] Naske & Slotnick, 110.
[88] Naske & Slotnick, 117.
[89] J. Arthur Lazell, *Alaskan Apostle: The Life Story of Sheldon Jackson* (New York: Harper & Brothers, 1960), 53.

designate funding for education in Alaska. It was this lobbying that ultimately resulted in the passage of the Organic Act, a provision of which set aside $25,000 to establish schools for the education of Alaskan children.[90] Jackson was appointed as general agent of education for Alaska, under the US Bureau of Education.[91]

Jackson used his government role to promote the cause of missions in Alaska. The $25,000 in government funding was woefully inadequate for the task at hand, and Jackson saw here an opportunity for the Church to become involved in educating Alaskan children. Through his encouragement and direction, at least six more denominations (in addition to the Orthodox and Presbyterians) were mobilized to establish schools (and by implication churches) in various parts of the state.

Though there is widely understood to have been an official "comity meeting" or "comity agreement" between these denominations, no specific record of such a meeting exists. Thomas places the date for the "meeting" in 1885, whereas Lazell dates it to 1880, prior to Jackson's appointment as education agent.[92] Considering the lack of official documentation and the variety of dates offered for the "meeting," it is perhaps best to follow Kurt Vitt in his suggestion that there was no actual "Comity Meeting" or official "Comity Agreement."[93] Rather, there seems to have existed in Jackson's strategic vision what might be appropriately called a "Comity Plan." As he appealed to the various individual denominations for missionaries and schoolteachers and directed them to various regions of the state, he had in his mind the idea to divide the state into various regions, each of which could be "assigned" to a particular group. Some groups, such as the Moravians, came to be a part of this "patchwork quilt" by specific invitation from Jackson, whereas others such as the Anglicans and Catholics came more of their own volition, naturally following the Yukon from their already-established missions upriver in Canada. Jackson, through his federal role (holding the purse strings for the education funding), was able to loosely oversee all of their efforts and to generally steer new denominations to the areas of greatest need, preventing overlap. As a result, by 1900, missionary work had been established along Alaska's entire coastline and the length of the Yukon River. Kurt Vitt provides a helpful chronology of the various denominations' arrival in Alaska through 1900:[94]

---

[90] Naske & Slotnick, 118.
[91] Lazell, 69-70.
[92] Tay Thomas, *Cry in the Wilderness* (Anchorage: Color Art, 1967), 35; Lazell, 65.
[93] James W. Henkelman & Kurt H. Vitt, *Harmonious to Dwell: The History of the Alaska Moravian Church, 1885-1985* (Bethel: Tundra, 1985), 33.
[94] Adapted from Henkelman & Vitt, 36 and Lazell, 65.

Table 3.1: Chronology of Denominational Missions in Alaska

Date	Denomination	Region
1794	Russian Orthodox	Aleutian Islands, Prince William Sound, and Southeast Panhandle
1877	Presbyterians	Southeast Panhandle, Arctic Coast
1885	Moravians	Kuskokwim River Delta
1886	Roman Catholics	Lower Yukon River
1886	Episcopalians	Upper Yukon River
1887	Quakers	Kotzebue Sound
1887[95]	Evangelical Covenant	Norton Sound
1889	Methodists	Aleutian Islands
1889	Baptists	Cook Inlet & Kodiak
1894	Lutherans	Cape Prince of Wales
1899	Salvation Army	Southeast Panhandle

In terms of the development of an indigenous church for Alaska, this recruitment and organization of the missionary force was the most notable and enduring contribution of Jackson and the Presbyterians. Jackson cast the vision and developed the infrastructure that would allow these denominations to become established. The educational system that he pioneered laid the foundation for many of these groups to train indigenous pastors to lead their own churches, to varying degrees of success.

By and large, the early Presbyterian missionaries on the field focused on evangelism and education of the Native children. This was accomplished primarily through elementary schools and residential children's homes. The vast need for education in the state coincided with a series of terrible epidemics in the late 1800s and early 1900s that took a disproportionate toll on Native communities. In what is remembered in Native oral tradition as "the Great Death," up to 60% of the Native population was lost, and children across the state were left without parents and placed into these residential homes run by the various Christian missions.[96] This pattern was established early on by the Presbyterians, and under Jackson's direction was replicated by others across

---

[95] Vitt dates the beginning of the Covenant work to 1889, but this is simply the date that the work was officially transferred from the Swedish Covenant to the American Covenant. The Swedish Covenant arrived in 1887.

[96] Harold Napoleon, *Yuuyaraq: The Way of the Human Being* (Fairbanks: Alaska Native Knowledge Network, 1996), 10.

the entire territory—nearly every mission established during this era operated at least one children's home.

Unfortunately, these schools and children's homes run by the Protestants and Roman Catholics generally did not follow in the philosophy of cultural contextualization that had been established by the Russian Orthodox predecessors. A spirit of paternalism, rather than indigenization, dominated the early Protestant efforts. The federal government saw education as a tool of cultural assimilation and used the missions as a means to "civilize" the indigenous peoples of the state. Under Jackson's leadership, the Bureau of Education sought to replace the local languages with English, and indigenous languages were not permitted in the schools.[97] Children in the church-run homes and schools were routinely punished for speaking in their own languages, and the abuse that too often characterized these ministries is well-documented in hindsight.[98]

Likely as a result of this paternalism, a strong indigenous leadership movement never resulted from the Presbyterian ministries. It was not until the 1940s that two Presbyterian Inupiat ministers were ordained—Percy Ipalook of Barrow (ordained 1941) and Roy Ahmaogak of Wainwright (1947).[99] Both were educated in Presbyterian seminaries outside Alaska.[100] Sheldon Jackson college was founded as a Presbyterian institution of higher education in Sitka, but this school focused primarily on industrial training and teacher education, with no seminary options.[101]

Alaska Bible Seminary (Moravian)

Not all of the mainline denominations that began work in Alaska in the 1890s followed in the Presbyterian pattern of cultural assimilation. The Moravian Church was the first denomination to answer Jackson's plea for missionaries to Alaska, and it also provides the sharpest contrast against the Presbyterian methodology.[102] The Moravian "Society for Propagating the Gospel Among the Heathen" received Jackson's request in 1883, and by 1885 the first missionaries, John and Edith Kilbuck and William and Caroline Weinland, were established on the banks of the Kuskokwim River at the site of present-day Bethel.[103]

The Moravian missionaries made a conscious and intentional effort to oppose the formal government policies against use of the indigenous languages.

---

[97] Henkelman & Vitt, 39.
[98] Napoleon, 13.
[99] Thomas, 67.
[100] Thomas, 67.
[101] Lazell, 210.
[102] Henkelman & Vitt, 32.
[103] Henkelman & Vitt, 89.

Ministry in the local vernacular had been a hallmark of the Moravian church since its inception during the European Reformations: "In order to serve Native peoples genuinely and with appropriate understanding, they were willing, as much as possible, to become like Natives, especially as far as language, clothing and food were concerned."[104] Thus, the Moravians produced the first Yupik Grammar & Dictionary within four years of beginning ministry, followed by a collection of catechisms, hymns, and liturgies in 1902, key portions of Scripture in 1928, and the complete New Testament in 1956.[105] The complete Yupik Bible was published in 2016.[106] Moravian historians reported in 1985, "Many of the Moravian Native Pastors, Laypastors, and Helpers have never become conversant in English. All of them, however, are fluent and literate in Yup'ik."[107]

The process of training these indigenous pastoral leaders began early in the Kilbucks' ministry. From the outset, the missionaries sought to identify individuals with leadership potential and to develop them for ministry. Five years after the mission began, in 1890, two Yupik men, David Skuviuk and George Nukachlak, were sponsored by the Moravian church to receive training in Carlisle, PA, near the Moravian headquarters there.[108] The men spent three years in training and returned to Bethel as interpreters and assistants to the missionaries.[109] Through this experience, the church realized that sending individuals far away for training was more problematic than beneficial and began to look for ways to develop leadership locally.

Vitt summarizes the methodology that the early missionaries employed: "It was the task of the individual missionary to seek out capable and interested Native men and train them on a personal one-to-one basis."[110] Many were identified as candidates for leadership through their time spent in the mission school, where special Bible classes for upper-level students "provided the special students with preparatory training for a future ministry."[111] These individuals, discipled by the missionaries through direct "on the job" ministry experience, became formally known as "Helpers" in Moravian polity. Vitt emphasizes, "In more recent years (1948) the designation 'lay pastor' has replaced the term 'Helper' in the Alaska Moravian Church. In short, calling the Native lay-ministers *Helpers* in those early years was not a 'put-down' or

---

[104] Henkelman & Vitt, 6.
[105] Henkelman & Vitt, 39.
[106] "Bible translated into modern Yup'ik," *Alaska Dispatch News*, 8 July 2016.
[107] Henkelman & Vitt, 39.
[108] Henkelman & Vitt, 375.
[109] Henkelman & Vitt, 375.
[110] Henkelman & Vitt, 375.
[111] Henkelman & Vitt, 375.

implying an inferior position, rather it was in keeping with Moravian tradition, philosophy of ministry, and the church vernacular."[112]

The first Moravian Helpers were named Lomuk and Kawagaleg, appointed in 1891. Helpers Skuviuk and Nukachaluk joined them when they returned from Pennsylvania in 1893, and Helper Neck was appointed in 1894.[113] Within nine years of ministry, then, a team of five lay pastors had already been established in the Moravian Church. A sixth—Helper Hooker—was martyred in 1890 at the hands of a boy suffering from what appears to have been demonization—"the only recorded incident of a Moravian being martyred along the Kuskokwim."[114]

These lay pastors were not confined to ministry under the watchful eye of the missionaries, but rather were dispatched on their own to far-flung villages up the river and along the coastline. Helper Kawagaleg was first sent to Akiak and subsequently to Quinhagak when no missionary could be found to work there. David Skuviuk was sent to Ogavik, and Neck to Napaskiak.[115]

Ongoing training was essential to support these novice workers, so "From time to time, the Helpers would meet with the Missionaries to obtain additional training and biblical instruction."[116] These "Helper Conferences" would generally meet for approximately five days of intensive instruction at least once per year.[117] By 1932, these training conferences had been extended to four weeks of instruction each winter and were renamed "The Helpers' Institute."[118] In 1945, the training program expanded further, becoming the "Helper Training School." However, even this permanent school did not follow traditional academic patterns:

> After sixty years of ministry among the Yup'ik, the missionaries were quite aware as to what they might or might not ask with respect to length of school terms. They recognized and appreciated the nomadic tendencies and subsistence requirements of the people, including those who would sign up as students for the ministry. They would need to have time to go hunting and fishing during the summer and fall seasons. That restricted the months available for study. [119]

The school was first located in Nunapitsinghak at the site of the Moravian Children's Home, and was later moved to Bethel and renamed "The Training

---

[112] Henkelman & Vitt, 374-375.
[113] Henkelman & Vitt, 375.
[114] Henkelman & Vitt, 208.
[115] Henkelman & Vitt, 211-212.
[116] Henkelman & Vitt, 212.
[117] Henkelman & Vitt, 215.
[118] Henkelman & Vitt, 377.
[119] Henkelman & Vitt, 378.

School for Native Ministers."[120] In 1948, it was renamed again to "The Alaska Moravian Bible School," and continues to operate today as "Alaska Bible Seminary."[121]

The school is unaccredited, though it has begun pursuing affiliate status with the Association for Biblical Higher Education. It continues to teach classes primarily in the modular format, allowing students to complete a full course during an intensive period of one or two weeks. A 28-course program culminates in a "Christian Leadership Certification," with an additional six-course program combined with a one-semester internship under the supervision of a pastor culminating in a "Pastoral Certification."[122] Yupik language instruction continues to be an emphasis in the school today, with 40% of the instructors speaking Yupik in a usual semester, and all being made aware of the importance of culturally-relevant teaching styles.[123]

This combination of early, non-traditional leadership training patterns and the embrace of the local Yupik language allowed the Moravians to become the most successful Protestant denomination in terms of developing an entirely Native pastorate. The church ordained the first Native men to the full pastorate in 1946: Lloyd Neck and James Kinegak.[124] By 1983, the Alaska Moravian Church could legitimately claim to be "an indigenous, selfgoverning, Native administered church," under the direction of an all-Native board, with a Native bishop, and all native pastors, with the exception of two white pastors serving the English-speaking congregations in Dillingham and Bethel.[125]

Alaska Christian College & Western Alaska Ministry Training (Evangelical Covenant)

The Evangelical Covenant work in Alaska began in 1887, two years after the Moravian mission was launched 200 miles to the south. Axel E. Karlson of the Swedish Covenant Church was the first missionary, and he established the ministry in the village of Unalakleet.[126] This village sat near the transition between traditionally Yupik territory to the south and Inupiat territory to the north, and eventually the Evangelical Covenant ministry expanded to include villages from both linguistic groups.

Like the Presbyterians and most other Protestant groups working in Alaska, the Covenant Church ministered primarily in English, working through

---

[120] Henkelman & Vitt, 378.
[121] Henkelman & Vitt, 379.
[122] *Alaska Bible Seminary Student Handbook* (Bethel: Alaska Bible Seminary, 2015), 16.
[123] Edward Dehnert, "Letter of reference," email to John Ferch, 9 May 2016.
[124] Henkelman & Vitt, 378.
[125] Henkelman & Vitt, 351.
[126] L. Arden Almquist, *Covenant Missions in Alaska* (Chicago: Covenant, 1962), 19.

interpreters.[127] To his credit, "Karlson gradually learned some Eskimo, and as he did, he would preach in a mixture of English and Eskimo."[128] Nevertheless, ministry in the local vernacular was not a major concern for the Covenant Church, and even the mid-twentieth century Covenant historian Arden Almquist argued that emphasizing Native language acquisition might "cause a tendency to retard transition to the inevitable day when English would replace it completely, with a constant rejection of the church by its youth."[129]

Although the Evangelical Covenant Church did not prioritize the use of indigenous languages, it demonstrated a marked difference from the Presbyterian approach in its attitude towards developing indigenous leadership. In this regard, its ministry has more closely resembled that of the Moravians. Indeed, though the English-speaking missionaries made little effort to learn Yupik or Inupiaq, they were not hesitant to allow and empower the Yupik and Inupiat believers to minister on their own. Uyagaq "Rock" was the first such individual, taken into the Karlsons' home as a youth after his father was murdered. Rock began accompanying Karlson on his "gospel journeys" in 1887, and by 1900 was "taken on as a Covenant missionary."[130] Others of note included Stephan Ivanoff (Karlson's first interpreter, appointed a deacon in 1892), his brother Misha Ivanoff (sent to Hooper Bay in 1927), Harry Soxie (Little Diomede, 1930), Jacob Kenick (Nunivak Island, 1936), Fred Savok (Elim, 1948), and still more who span the decades and are too numerous to list.[131]

It was in 1919 that "the first truly indigenous work began" with the ordination of Wilson Gonangnan, the first Inuit pastor to be ordained by the Evangelical Covenant Church.[132] L. E. Ost had been advocating since 1915 to put "the work in the native's hand," and together with Lars Almquist ordained Gonangnan to establish a new work in the Yupik community of Mountain Village.[133] Though Almquist hints that this ordination may not have been consistent with formal Covenant polity, it was in every way consistent with the Pauline model offered in Scripture.[134] Notably, Gonangnan's work in Mountain Village was financed entirely by the Inuit church.[135] It is quite possible that Gonangnan was the first Alaskan Inuk to be ordained as clergy, though it should

---

[127] Almquist, 21.
[128] Almquist, 21.
[129] Almquist, 152.
[130] Almquist, 49. Almquist follows an older spelling, "Ayachak," for his Inupiaq name, which means "Rock."
[131] Almquist, 35-36, 48-54.
[132] Almquist, 36.
[133] Almquist, 149.
[134] Almquist, 149.
[135] Almquist, 149

be noted that Gonangnan is remembered today in official Covenant records as a "lay pastor."[136]

These individuals have been trained for ministry through a variety of means over the years. Some of the earliest, such as Rock and Ivanoff, were discipled directly by Karlson as they interpreted for him and accompanied him on his trips. Later, Almquist describes how missionaries such as L. E. Ost "had Bible training for Eskimo pastors off and on during the years."[137] In 1948, a small Bible institute was established in Unalakleet that operated for a number of years, though in 1962 Almquist perceived that this institute was no longer sustainable with only five students.[138] Instead, Almquist suggested several alternatives, including sending candidates out of state to the denomination's North Park Theological Seminary in Illinois, working with other organizations providing cross-denominational training in-state, or establishing some form of local training through correspondence or modular coursework facilitated by visiting teachers.[139]

In subsequent years, the denomination has employed all of these methods to varying degrees of success. The current director of the Alaska Conference of the Evangelical Covenant Church, Curtis Ivanoff of Unalakleet, is a 2008 graduate of North Park Theological Seminary.[140] During the 1970s and 1980s, several individuals from the Covenant churches attended Arctic Bible Institute, run by InterAct Ministries in Palmer.[141] More recently, several have attended Alaska Bible College and LEaD Alaska.

In 2000, the denomination established Alaska Christian College (ACC), a two-year school in Soldotna, Alaska, accredited by the Association for Biblical Higher Education. ACC offers an Associate of Arts degree in Christian Ministry, but this does not lead to licensing or ordination. Rather, it is designed "to provide students with knowledge and skills necessary for entry-level employment and to prepare students to transfer to a baccalaureate program."[142] Associate Superintendent James Barefoot reported that many students enter ACC not having a saving relationship with Jesus Christ, and the

---

[136] Eva Malvich, "Native Missionaries in Rural Alaska," *Friends of Covenant History* (Summer/Fall 2015), 7.
[137] Almquist, 64.
[138] Almquist, 65.
[139] Almquist, 153.
[140] "Alumni Profile: Curtis Ivanoff S'08," *North Park Theological Seminary*, www.northpark.edu/seminary/academics/dual-degrees/master-of-arts-christian-ministry-and-mba-or-mna/alumni-profile-curtis-ivanoff-s08/ (Accessed 24 August 2017).
[141] Clarence "Barney" Furman, *Serving by God's Power in the North*, pre-release copy (Boring: InterAct, 2017), 99-100.
[142] *Alaska Christian College Academic Catalog 2020-2021* (Soldotna: Alaska Christian College, 2020), 30.

school excels at leading students to faith, helping them overcome academic challenges, and preparing them for further studies.[143] Some are challenged to enter ministry through this process, and graduates of ACC who are interested in preparation as ministers may transfer directly to BA programs at Alaska Bible College or North Park University through articulation agreements with these schools.

For many years, a seminary degree was a requirement for full ordination in the Covenant Church, which meant that any Inuit pastor seeking ordination must ultimately complete graduate studies at North Park Theological Seminary—an enormous barrier considering the great cultural distance between Chicago and Western Alaska. In 2010, a group of Alaskan Covenant leaders developed an alternative path to ordination that would provide the necessary training for an Alaskan pastor in a culturally-relevant context.[144] This track was titled "Western Alaska Ministry Training" (WAMT). The program follows the same "modular" format used with success by the Moravians, meeting twice per year for five days of intensive instruction. The fifteen-course program takes seven years to complete at this pace. According to James Barefoot, "This works well for village people who have other jobs, families and subsistence that demand most of their time."[145] In a sense, through WAMT, the Covenant Church has returned to the training model that was employed effectively by its earliest Alaskan missionaries—occasional, intensive training modules designed to support those already active in ministry roles.

Today, the Evangelical Covenant Church struggles, like most other denominations, to appoint indigenous leadership. At least five village churches have been without pastors for some time. However, this tide may be turning slowly. The appointment of Curtis Ivanoff as Director of the Alaska Conference is certainly a move in the right direction, and several promising Inuit individuals from Covenant churches are actively pursuing training through Alaska Bible College, LEaD Alaska, and Western Alaska Ministry Training.

Friends Bible Training School (Friends)

The Friends, or Quakers, arrived in Alaska in 1887. Their earliest ministry focused on the Tlingit people of the Southeast panhandle where the Presbyterians already had an established ministry. At the encouragement of Sheldon Jackson, their focus was redirected to the Inupiat people of the

---

[143] LEaD Alaska, *Governance Council Meeting*, 31 July 2017.
[144] James Barefoot, "WAMT," email to John Ferch, 10 August 2017.
[145] Barefoot, "WAMT."

Northwest coast around Kotzebue Sound, with the work in Southeast Alaska being turned over to the Presbyterians.[146]

On the Northwest coast, the Friends made notable strides towards development of an indigenous pastorate, which in many ways paralleled the work of the Evangelical Covenant, 200 miles to the south. Both working among the Inupiat who shared mutually intelligible dialects, a good degree of "cross-pollination" occurred between the two ministries over the years. In fact, it was the early Inupiaq Covenant missionary Uyagaq Rock who established the gospel in Kotzebue Sound in 1893.[147] These early believers appealed to Sheldon Jackson for missionaries to help them grow in their faith, and Jackson directed them to the Friends, who relocated to Kotzebue Sound in 1897.[148]

Having heard the gospel from one of their own people, the idea of Native preachers was not strange to the early believers of Kotzebue Sound, and indigenous leaders such as Whittier Williams emerged as early as 1903.[149] As in the Covenant Church, these early leaders had often been introduced to ministry through their role as interpreters.[150] The Caucasian Friends missionaries took a bilingual approach, with the schoolteachers particularly emphasizing the use of English, but others learning and ministering in Inupiaq.[151]

Wilson Cox, who served as superintendent of the ministry from 1909-1912, established plans for a summer Bible Training School in Kotzebue, which "consisted of three-hour sessions each evening, four nights a week, from the end of the yearly meeting until the time people had to return upriver."[152] This summer school continued until in 1947, when a more permanent school was established in Noorvik.[153] The school was moved to Kotzebue in 1970.[154] David Miller, who directed this school most recently until his retirement in 2016, describes the training format:

> The school would run from the end of September to the first part of March. The classes were from 9 AM to 12 PM Monday through Friday. They would study one subject at a time for 1, 2 or 3 weeks, depending on the amount of material to be covered. This type of schedule is a benefit for bringing in different teachers to teach specific classes for that period. With different teachers there are varieties of teaching methods. This gives the student a

---

[146] Arthur O. Roberts, *Tomorrow is Growing Old: Stories of the Quakers in Alaska* (Newberg: Barclay, 1978), 162, 81.
[147] Roberts, 154.
[148] Roberts, 162.
[149] Roberts, 215.
[150] Roberts, 215
[151] Roberts, 208-209.
[152] Roberts, 228, 231.
[153] Roberts, 353.
[154] Roberts, 354.

broader range of instruction. It also allows those that have only a week or two available to be able to attend a whole class.[155]

Though this school closed in 2016, it provides yet another example of how non-traditional academic patterns can be used effectively to train Inuit leaders.

"Gospel trips" were also important to the Friends' success in developing Inuit pastors:

> A gospel trip consisted of a group of people from one village going on a ministry of visitation to another village. They would preach and sing and pray together. The gospel trip uniquely blended Eskimo nomadic travel and Quaker concern for the ministry of every Christian. From time immemorial the people had followed a rhythm of travel associated with the cycles of subsistence.[156]

The Friends' relatively "low church" ecclesiology, which emphasizes the priesthood of all believers, encouraged many Inupiat believers to become personally involved in ministry prior to becoming what some would call "fully trained" in a seminary context. According to Miller, "From this training, many of the native people went out into full-time service for the Lord. There were native pastors in each of the nine villages of the area."[157]

Alaska Bible College (SEND North)

The arrival of the twentieth century brought the Fundamentalist/Modernist controversy to American shores. The movement of many of the "mainline denominations" towards a "social gospel" of love and good works had great ramifications on Christian missions globally, and Alaska was no exception.[158] As several of the established Alaskan missions moved in a more ecumenical direction that tended to deemphasize evangelism and church planting in favor of education and medical ministry, the scene was set for another great wave of Alaskan missions—the independent mission agencies. Though churches had been established in Alaska's coastal villages and along the Yukon River artery during the second wave under Jackson's comity plan, the vast interior region south of the Yukon remained largely untouched by the gospel. Two major independent, nondenominational mission agencies were formed to fill this void: Central Alaskan Missions (today known as SEND North) and Arctic Missions (today known as InterAct Ministries). Both agencies founded schools that contributed immensely to the training of Inuit leaders during the second half of the twentieth century.

---

[155] David Miller, "Friends Bible Training School," email to John Ferch, 8 August 2017.
[156] Roberts, 370.
[157] Miller, "Friends Bible Training School," email.
[158] Neill, 419.

Central Alaskan Missions was born out of the vision of one man—Vincent James Joy—who incorporated the mission in New Jersey and moved his family to Copper Center, Alaska, in 1937. Having longed to serve in Alaska since high school, Joy had learned of the need in the Copper River Basin from an Episcopal priest who visited Moody Bible Institute while Joy was enrolled as a student.[159] A visionary and an entrepreneur, Vince Joy was quick to recruit more missionaries to the cause. Though governed by a board, Joy was the board's leader and set the tone and vision for the entire mission.[160] The early work of Central Alaskan Missions (CAM) was focused on the Ahtna Athabaskan region of interior Alaska. Several Ahtna churches were planted, and an informal, nonresidential "Native Bible School" successfully trained four Ahtna men as pastors.[161]

By 1958, CAM had begun to envision a resident Bible School in Glennallen.[162] It is not clear whether this was intended to replace or complement the existing non-residential Native Bible School, but what is clear is that Joy intended the finished product to look very different from what was already in operation. Ever a "builder" (metaphorically and literally), Joy became increasingly focused on the mission's role in the economic development of the booming region towards the end of his life and ministry.[163] Thus, he insisted that the residential school should be a formally accredited Bible college, following a traditional four-year academic pattern and granting a bachelor's degree.[164] He wrote to the Alaska Commissioner of Education, "We feel that Alaska needs a college-level school where young people may obtain liberal arts as well as a thorough study of the Word of God."[165] Not all of CAM agreed with Joy in this vision, and in 1960 the rest of the board issued him a letter of censure, pointing out that in Joy's fundraising efforts, "What is presented as mission plans and developments is only personal."[166] In fact, some of the missionaries felt so strongly that "the college concept, rather than just a Bible school" was the wrong decision that they ultimately resigned from the mission.[167]

As was usually the case, Joy's visionary persistence won out in the end, and Alaska Bible College opened its doors in September 1966. Tragically, Joy himself died that August, just prior to the college's opening, as the result of a

---

[159] Faye Crandall, *Into the Copper River Valley: The Letters and Ministry of Vincent James Joy, Pioneer Missionary to Alaska* (Taylors: Faith, 1994), 32.
[160] Crandall, 99.
[161] Crandall, 142.
[162] Crandall, 135.
[163] Crandall, 223.
[164] Crandall, 147.
[165] Crandall, 230.
[166] Crandall, 149.
[167] Crandall, 161; Bob Lee, personal conversation with author, Palmer, 27 October 2016.

rapid degenerative brain condition that was likely triggered by a bulldozer accident that occurred while clearing land for the college several months prior.[168] Nevertheless, the school did open, and the activities of the Native Bible School came to an end just three years later, in 1969.[169]

The college's first graduate was Rose (Charley) Tyone, a local Ahtna woman who was the daughter of Walter Charley, one of the four Ahtna pastors mentioned earlier.[170] Rose went on to earn a master's degree from Talbot Seminary and served for many years as a missionary to Native Americans in the American Southwest before returning to Alaska. She and her husband Lonnie are now respected elders in the community and continue to serve the Gulkana village church. However, Rose became the exception rather than the rule, as for the first twenty years of its existence the college failed to produce many indigenous leaders in comparison to its predecessor, the Native Bible School. Gaining accreditation (granted in 1982) was always a major focus, and the college closely followed the traditional academic patterns expected of a degree-granting institution and therefore attracted primarily Caucasian students from Alaska and the Lower 48. Contributing to this trend was the competition from Arctic Bible Institute, another residential Bible school that also opened in 1966 and catered primarily to Native learners.

In the 1990s, this trend began to shift. The Arctic Bible Institute's residential component closed in 1989, shortly after Gary Ridley was appointed ABC's fourth president in 1988. Ridley was pursuing a Doctor of Missiology degree at the time, and contextualization was the focus of his dissertation—particularly, contextualization of leadership for Alaska Native churches. The result of this dissertation was a paradigm for biblical leadership in Alaska Native culture, which he sought to apply to the curriculum at Alaska Bible College.[171] In 1998, the Board of Directors wrote this into the ten-year vision statement for the school:

> At the Glennallen campus, the Native American presence is growing as ABC develops and intentionally structures its learning environment in order to minister to Native Americans in a culturally relevant and sensitive manner. In both residential and distance education context, new pathways to learning are developed in order to better equip and educate the Native American for ministry in the village church.[172]

---

[168] Crandall, 242.
[169] Lee, conversation.
[170] "Commencement Program" (Glennallen: Alaska Bible College, 1970).
[171] Ridley, 103-104.
[172] "Vision for Alaska Bible College, 1998," Board document (Glennallen: Alaska Bible College 2002).

Though the academic structure of the college has remained largely unchanged, the school sought to become more "native-friendly" in campus life and recruitment of students.[173]

In 2010, the college became independent of its parent organization, SEND North (CAM having merged with the Far Eastern Gospel Crusade to form what is now SEND International in 1971).[174] With this change, the college implemented a new strategic plan to emphasize recruitment of Alaskan students, including Alaska Natives. The college moved from Glennallen to Palmer in 2013—a move that put the school "within easy driving distance of 40% of the entire state's population," including state's the largest population of Alaska Natives.[175] The college also began developing a distance education program, with the stated goal "that people in rural communities will not have to leave their villages for four years to get a Bible education."[176] Since moving to Palmer, the college has developed a greater level of partnership with other Native-focused ministries throughout the state, establishing articulation agreements with Alaska Christian College and Tanalian Leadership Center, and helping to administer the not-for-credit LEaD Alaska residential discipleship program. These shifts over the past thirty years have resulted in a gradual increase in the enrollment of Alaska Native students, including several from Inuit communities. During my (John) six-year tenure, the school enrolled one Inupiaq and three Yupik students. Nevertheless, recruitment efforts and instructional methods continue to target traditional students, and the majority of ABC's students continue to come from a Caucasian background.

Arctic Bible Institute (InterAct Ministries)

InterAct Ministries was established in September of 1951, under the name "Alaska Missions, Inc." To avoid confusion or conflict with other agencies, the name was changed in 1956 to "Arctic Missions," which was used until the current name, "InterAct Ministries," was adopted in 1988.[177] John Gillespie, a close friend and colleague of Vince Joy, was the impetus behind InterAct's founding. However, Gillespie's vision was not to start a new work from scratch in the manner of Vince Joy and CAM, but rather to network the large number of independent missionaries already working in Southcentral Alaska so that they could benefit from pooled resources and develop a unified strategy for reaching

---

[173] Alaska Bible College, *Meeting with Administrators and Roger Huntington*, 20 April 1999.
[174] Untitled article, *NorthWord: A Publication of Alaska Bible College* (Fall 2010), 1.
[175] *Alaska Bible College Academic Catalog 2017-2018* (Palmer: Alaska Bible College, 2017), 11.
[176] Michelle Eastty, "Ferches join faculty," *NorthWord: A Publication of Alaska Bible College* (Summer 2012), 7.
[177] *InterAct Ministries Member Handbook* (Boring: InterAct Ministries, 2007), 8.

Alaska.[178] Sixteen independent missionaries initially joined the new mission.[179] With CAM focused on the eastern interior region of the Copper River Valley, Arctic Missions focused on the western interior, its ministries ranging from Lakes Clark and Iliamna in the west to the Talkeetna Mountains in the east, and from the Yukon River in the north to the Kenai Peninsula and Kodiak Island in the south. While CAM/SEND often struggled with issues pertaining to its top-down leadership style, InterAct has more often struggled as a mission run from the "bottom up," with its roots not in the heart of a single visionary, but rather in a "confederation" of independent missionaries that each shared a slightly different perspective on the needs of Alaska and the methods best suited to meet those needs.

One of Arctic Missions' earliest ministries that developed entirely "in house" (rather than beginning as an independent work later incorporated into the mission) was Victory High School (VHS), established in 1959.[180] The school was housed at Victory Bible Camp in the Talkeetna Mountains, midway between Palmer and Glennallen. (The camp had been formed independently by Vince Joy and John Gillespie several years prior to Arctic Missions being founded and later became part of the new mission.[181]) The residential high school "was established to offer a Christ-centered education to Christian natives so that they would be prepared to teach others, especially their own people."[182] Native students boarded at VHS from around the state.

Since the vision of the school from the outset was to train Christians to teach their own people, this naturally led to establishment of a Bible institute that could provide further training to those high school graduates sensing a call to ministry. Thus, Arctic Bible Institute (ABI) opened with seven students at Victory Bible Camp in 1966 (the same year that Alaska Bible College opened in Glennallen).[183] Together, VHS and ABI formed the "Arctic Training Center."[184] In 1972, with the closure of the Lazy Mountain Children's Home in Palmer, that campus was donated to the mission and became the new home of ABI (with VHS remaining at Victory Bible Camp until its closure in 1982).[185]

Through 1988, ABI utilized a residential model that followed a traditional semester calendar. However, the school also incorporated "gospel teams" into the calendar to involve the students in ministry during their training. ABI instructor George Schultz described this ministry:

---

[178] Furman, 6.
[179] Furman, 8.
[180] Furman, 89.
[181] Crandall, 106.
[182] Furman, 88.
[183] Furman, 92.
[184] Furman, 93.
[185] Furman, 93

> Each February [the Gospel Teams] take a 10-day trip to selected villages. This year [1985] we sent one team to some of the Bering Sea Eskimo villages and I led the other team to the interior Indian villages. We managed to get in on the coldest part of the winter with temperatures dipping to -63 F. Despite the cold, many came to our meetings; and we had the privilege of staying in their homes.... On the way home from one of our recent trips one student commented, "These trips sure are good. I really grow in my Christian walk as I share my testimony."[186]

The residential model was effective in training Native leaders over the years, who came from many different denominational backgrounds. Henkelman & Vitt summarize participation from the Moravian church:

> Alice and Sophie Coolidge, Wassilie and Jean Mute, Jonas Anaver, and Arthur Coolidge, attended the Arctic Bible Institute in Palmer, AK for three years each, since the Moravian Bible Seminary did not provide for year-round training. Lucie Coolidge had already attended the ABI for four years in the sixties, and quite a number of Moravian girls went for just one year. It was not common at the time for women to attend the Moravian Bible Seminary.[187]

Many from the Evangelical Covenant Church also attended, including Jerry & Lucy Daniels, who served in the pastorate in Hooper Bay, Unalakleet, and Golovin.[188]

In 1988, the residential component of ABI closed due to declining enrollment. Gale Van Diest, General Director of InterAct Ministries at the time, attributes the decline to a failure to fit the curriculum to the timeframe of the Native culture, and too much concern for "accreditation requirements."[189] (Though the program was not accredited, it did fall under the oversight of the Alaska Commission on Postsecondary Education, which required a certain amount of classroom hours.[190]) The school shifted to an extension model, offering training through correspondence and through weeklong modules held on-site in Native villages.[191] These modules gradually came to an end as well. Former ABI director George Schultz suggests that lack of leadership was a contributing factor in this decline.[192] Staffing the program was a consistent challenge for InterAct, and ABI went through at least eight different directors

---

[186] Furman, 93.
[187] Henkelman & Vitt, 381.
[188] Furman, 99-100.
[189] InterAct Ministries, *Lazy Mountain Consultation Team Meeting*, 22 July 2013.
[190] George Schultz, "History of ABI," email to John Ferch, 23 August 2017.
[191] Furman, 95.
[192] Schultz, "History of ABI."

from 1966 through the early '90s (for comparison, Alaska Bible College saw only four different presidents during the same period).[193] ABI never officially "closed," but was eventually rebranded as "InterAct Ministries Resource Center" to provide "training resources for native Alaskan Christians."[194]

Recent Developments in Alaska (Training Partnerships)

Since the closure of its residential school, InterAct has struggled to train Native leaders just as most of the other churches and missions have in recent years. Barney Furman writes, "Some [InterAct] villages have had active indigenous churches, but now proceed very slowly. Most villages are small, with very few leaders."[195] Recognizing this challenge, in 2013 the mission formed a Consultation Team to develop a strategy for the future of the Lazy Mountain property. Alaska Bible College, Alaska Freedom Journey, Arctic Barnabas, the Evangelical Covenant Church, and InterAct Ministries were all represented on the Consultation Team. Through collaborative research, the Consultation Team concluded that each of the ministries represented is seeing the same challenges that InterAct faces in developing Native leadership—the previous generation of Native leaders is in decline, and no organization is seeing widespread success in developing a new generation of pastors.[196]

This led to the development of the LEaD Alaska residential discipleship program in 2016, "a collaboration of ministries sharing a desire to see followers of Jesus discipled as Christian leaders who will impact their communities for Christ, with a particular focus on Alaska Natives."[197] LEaD operates on a winter-only calendar to allow time for culturally-important subsistence activities in the summer and fall. During the winter months, each organization takes turns providing various training modules and activities for the students. Modules are planned to provide a holistic approach to ministry, emphasizing four components: life skills, biblical training, emotional healing, and cultural worldview understanding. Some students attend for the entire time, while others come only for particular modules. Through Alaska Bible College's participation, earning academic credit is an option for students, but not required. Key to the entire program is a "relational… approach [that] will allow us to individualize extensively to best meet the needs of participants."[198]

The formation of LEaD Alaska may signal the beginning of a fourth "wave" of missions in Alaska—the era of partnership. In the development of LEaD, each organization acknowledged its own shortcomings and failures in developing

---

[193] Furman, 92-93, 115-116.
[194] *InterAct Ministries Member Handbook*, 8.
[195] Furman, 43.
[196] InterAct Ministries, *Lazy Mountain Consultation Team Meeting*, 22 July 2013.
[197] "LEaD Alaska Memorandum of Understanding" (Palmer: LEaD Alaska, 2016), 1.
[198] Furman, 106.

Native pastors, and affirmed each other's strengths. The vision for LEaD is that by working together, each organization can bring its own strength to the table in order to develop a culturally-relevant discipleship program to complement each ministry's existing programs.[199]

Concurrently to the development of LEaD, several other non-formal, lay-level approaches to leadership development have begun to emerge out of similar ministry partnership discussions. Tanalian Leadership Center is a program developed at Tanalian Bible Camp (another branch of the InterAct "family tree"). The program operates on a similar structure to LEaD, hosting students at its rural campus in Port Alsworth from October to May, where they participate in a program of Bible study, career development, and personal mentoring.[200]

Great Commission Alaska is another newcomer to the leadership development scene, providing a discipleship program for Alaska Native men recently released from the criminal justice system at their remote Kings Lodge facility. This program emphasizes "constructive work training, biblical counseling, and mentoring in God's word." [201] Great Commission Alaska operates in partnership with other organizations including Kokrine Hills Bible Camp, Native Brothers Restored, and Pioneers USA.[202]

Though promising, it is too early to evaluate the long-term success of these recently-emerging programs. All seem to emphasize common features including mentorship, job skills training, and Bible study. Notably, all of them are built around the same residential model that is in use by established Alaskan ministries such as Alaska Bible College, Alaska Christian College, and Alaska Bible Seminary, extracting individuals from their communities for an extended period of study at a central location. With the possible exception of Western Alaska Ministry Training (which emphasizes modular training), the earlier models of on-site training that were pioneered by the Moravians, the Evangelical Covenant Church, Friends, and CAM have fallen out of use.

Canada

Though the Christian faith has an enduring history in Canada dating to the late 1400s, the northern regions inhabited by the Inuit laid relatively untouched until much later in the nation's history. It was not until 1771 that a

---

[199] InterAct Ministries, *Lazy Mountain Consultation Team Meeting*, 9 September 2013.
[200] "Tanalian Leadership Center," *Tanalian Bible Camp*, http://tanalianleadershipcenter.org (Accessed 9 November 2020).
[201] "Discipleship Program," *Great Commission Alaska*, https://www.akmission.org/discipleship-program (Accessed 9 November 2020).
[202] Billy Tjernlund, "What are you going to do in Alaska?" Facebook, 5 February 2019, https://www.facebook.com/groups/thetjernlundtjournal/permalink/2000384313364729.

Moravian outreach was established among the southernmost Inuit of Labrador.[203] These Moravian congregations remain, but unlike the Alaskan Moravian Province, they have remained a "Mission Province" of the Unitas Fratrum (the worldwide body of Moravian churches) and have not developed an independent indigenous leadership training ministry.[204] The majority of the Canadian Inuit were Christianized through intense competition between the Anglican and Roman Catholic churches, which began their works among the Inuit in 1876 and 1912, respectively.[205] Most of the Canadian Inuit today identify nominally with one of these traditions. However, like in Greenland, actual rates of church attendance and religious observance are minimal. In 2009, Anthony Casey led a team to conduct a missiological ethnography of Iqaluit, the largest community and only city in the territory of Nunavut. This team found that the Anglican congregation claimed 6,000 adherents, or 90% of the city's population, while weekly church attendance averaged 500.[206] The missiologists' conversation with the local Anglican priest is telling of the spiritual condition of the Anglican Church in Nunavut:

> Towards the end of our conversation, the team member asked him [the priest] what he believed to be necessary for salvation. He said he did not know. When pressed as to what he would say if asked, "What must I do to be saved?" He said he would respond to come to his 9:45 Sunday service, watch carefully, and ask questions about anything that was not understood.[207]

Care must be taken here not to negate or delegitimatize sincere and orthodox expressions of faith that are present in both the Anglican and Roman Catholic traditions (as well as the Danish Lutheran tradition discussed earlier). Wherever possible, Evangelical ministries must work with, and not against, these established churches. However, the widespread nominalism and dependence on works for personal salvation among the Inuit cannot be ignored, and we cannot simply hope that Evangelical revitalization movements within these traditions will be sufficient to address the spiritual need in Northern Canada.

Historically, Northern Canada Evangelical Mission (NCEM) provided one of the earliest Evangelical outreaches among the Canadian Inuit. Gleason Ledyard and his wife Kathryn founded the ministry as Eskimo Gospel Crusade and began

---

[203] Frédéric B. Laugrand & Jarich G. Oosten, *Inuit Shamanism and Christianity: Transitions and Transformation in the Twentieth Century* (Montreal: McGill-Queen's, 2010). 37.
[204] "Directory of the Mission Provinces," *Unitas Fratrum*, http://www.unitasfratrum.org/index.php/mission-provinces/ (Accessed 26 October 2020).
[205] Laugrand & Oosten, 37.
[206] Antony Casey, ed., *Iqaluit Ethnography* (unpublished missiological ethnography, North American Mission Board, 2009). 19.
[207] Casey, 19.

their ministry around Hudson Bay in 1946.[208] The Ledyards encountered the same legalistic attitude towards salvation that Casey and his team reported many years later: "One of the hardest things to combat was the false idea that being baptized, conforming to church rules and rituals, and reading the same prayers morning and night was the essence of the Christian life."[209] The Ledyards worked among the Inuit for fifteen years and eventually produced the New Life Version, a translation of the Bible in simplified English designed for Inuit and First Nations people who spoke English as a second language.[210] More recently, however, NCEM has shifted its emphasis towards Canada's First Nations people, and though the Inuit are still mentioned in its promotional materials, the organization lists only one missionary, Ruth Armstrong, still serving full-time among the Inuit as public school teacher in Puvirnituq, Nunavik.[211]

SEND North

SEND North has operated in Canada since the days of CAM and Vince Joy (who surveyed Dawson City for a church plant in 1961), but historically this ministry has focused on First Nations communities in Yukon and British Colombia.[212] As the organization shifted its focus in Alaska away from the interior Athabaskans towards the coastal Yupik Inuit in the early 2000s, its leadership began to consider expanding their scope to include the Canadian Inuit of the Northwest Territories and Nunavut. In 2014, SEND established a missionary couple in Yellowknife, Northwest Territories, to provide a centralized base to support this expansion.[213] With no missionaries yet living full-time in Inuit communities, this work is still in infancy, and the most concrete ministry plans focus on evangelism rather than leadership development. Following SEND North's contemporary focus in Western Alaska, the organization's stated strategy is to "help Christian teachers and health workers move into these communities where they form relationships, start Bible studies, and lead people to Christ."[214] According to SEND North area director Jim Stamberg, the field does not currently endorse or prescribe a specific approach to leadership development, but it is expected to occur

---

[208] Tucker, 405.
[209] Gleason H. Ledyard, *And to the Eskimos* (Chicago: Moody, 1958). 162.
[210] Gleason & Kathryn Ledyard, "Introduction," in *Holy Bible - Old and New Testaments: New Life Version* (Uhrichsville: Barbour, 2014).
[211] "Armstrong, Ruth," *Northern Canada Evangelical Mission*, https://ncem.ca/missionaries/ruth-armstrong/ (Accessed 21 October 2020).
[212] Crandall, 158.
[213] "Reflection on Yellowknife 2014," *SEND International*, https://send.org/story/reflection-on-yellowknife-2014/. (Accessed 21 October 2020).
[214] "Eastward Expansion," *SEND North: Making Northern Disciple-makers* (Winter 2018). 1.

organically through these bivocational connections, with an emphasis on "story/oral focused methods and personal mentorship."[215]

Ethnos360

The spiritual conditions that the NAMB missiologists encountered in Iqaluit in 2009 remain relatively unchanged from what my (John's) father found when he surveyed the community with his coworker Ron Hiebert for New Tribes Mission in 1990. Shortly thereafter, NTM's field leadership in Greenland began laying plans to send a team to Iqaluit as an extension of the work happening across the Davis Strait in Greenland. Their own visas to remain in Greenland having been denied, my parents were hopeful to lead this team themselves.[216] However, NTM's Canadian office determined at the time that this work was unnecessary, since under the presiding missiology of the day, Canada was considered a "sending nation" rather than a mission field.[217]

In 2017, the organization, since renamed Ethnos360, reconsidered this position and launched a new field of ministry to focus on the Inuit and First Nations in northern Canada under the name "FirstStory Ministries."[218] This was originally branded as "a church planting partnership between Ethnos360 and NCEM."[219] In 2019, the FirstStory branding and NCEM's name were removed from the organization's Internet presence at www.firststoryministries.ca, which now redirects to Ethnos Canada's organizational website. These changes in leadership, as well as the global COVID-19 pandemic of 2020, have delayed the development of this new effort, but field director Shaun Humphreys reported that one family has plans to begin work in the Nunavik area of northern Quebec as soon as conditions allow.[220] These missionaries plan to use the same chronological Bible storying curriculum that Ethnos360 has used in Greenland as well as in Canadian First Nations contexts.[221]

Summary

In the 300 years since the gospel first came to the Inuit through the ministry of Hans Egede, the church has taken many different approaches to leadership development. Across the Arctic, Evangelical ministries have used methods

---

[215] Jim Stamberg, "NWT/Nunavut Update," email to John Ferch, 21 October 2020.
[216] Gary & Donna Ferch, "From Missionaries Gary and Donna Ferch," missionary prayer letter, January 1991.
[217] Gary Ferch, personal conversation with author, St. Louis, 24 October 2020.
[218] Ken Dewar, "Inuit ministry," email to John Ferch, 28 February 2019.
[219] Jason Bechtel, "Moving into Northern Canada," *NTM@work* (June 2017), https://ethnos.ca/moving-into-northern-canada/.
[220] Shaun Humphreys, "Inuit Ministry," email to John Ferch, 13 July 2020.
[221] Humphreys, "Inuit Ministry"; Dave Wright, "Establish OMC," *Osler Mission Chapel*, https://establishomc.blogspot.com (Accessed 7 December 2020).

ranging from one-on-one discipleship to formally accredited Bible college and seminary programs to train ministry leaders. These are summarized here from geographic and methodological perspectives.

Geographically speaking, Evangelical approaches to ministry leadership development are most widespread in Alaska due to the historical developments that gave Evangelical ministries a prominent role in the evangelization of the state. As Evangelical mission strategy has come to emphasize the importance of indigenous church leadership in recent years, these efforts have blossomed even further. Greenland has had a small but enduring Evangelical missionary presence since the 1980s. Though the work has been slow, it has begun to bear some fruit as Inuit believers progress through Ethnos360's foundational bible teaching curriculum and through one-on-one training with the INO. In Canada, Evangelical outreach has been slowest to take root among the Inuit due to the Anglican and Roman Catholic influence in the region. Two new Evangelical ministries have been established in the region during the past six years, but these are still in the pre-evangelism stage and have not yet established mechanisms for leadership development.

In terms of methodology, the most successful leadership training efforts over the years have been those that are embedded in the local community, employ a high degree of hands-on ministry experience, and are highly contextualized to the local language and culture. Recent years have seen the emergence of narrative-based approaches to the Bible as a particularly successful means of theological training.

Despite having made these strides towards a successful model for Inuit ministry leadership development, Evangelical churches and ministries continue to struggle with the task. No contemporary approach is consistently training leaders through a contextualized model that incorporates all of these "success factors." Ethnos360 offers a strong narrative-based approach to biblical education but has offered few opportunities for hands-on ministry experience. Programs such as Alaska Bible College, Western Alaska Ministry Training, and Alaska Bible Seminary offer strong Bible teaching and theological education modules, but they are often taught using traditional Western approaches by visiting pastors and missionaries. Nontraditional programs such as LEaD Alaska and Tanalian Leadership Center offer highly experiential approaches, but they too lack the oversight of local churches when students return home from a period of training. An integrated model for ministry leadership development in Inuit contexts has yet to be developed. Such a model will not replace the efforts surveyed in this chapter, but rather "connect the dots" by enabling each of them to identify areas in which they are lacking and providing a framework that will allow them to fill those gaps. It is to this task that the next chapter turns, beginning with an ethnological survey of Inuit leadership development.

Chapter 4
Ethnology of Inuit Leadership Development

Introduction

Our historical survey of leadership development efforts among the Inuit has revealed several preliminary "success factors," as well as a number of pitfalls that have influenced the process over the years. Though some approaches have proven more effective than others, these have all been informed primarily through the tension between longstanding Western academic norms and the practical realities of life and ministry in the Far North. A truly contextualized model for leadership development among the Inuit has yet to be developed.

In order to develop such a model, a detailed study of circumpolar Inuit cultures is needed. In chapter 2, we identified three key areas of culture that have particular bearing on the leadership development process: education, leadership, and social control. In this chapter, each of these areas of culture are examined in sequence using ethnographic data from representative communities across Alaska, Canada, and Greenland. This study of Inuit cultures will reveal common values pertaining to leadership development that will in turn allow us to develop a culturally appropriate model.

Inuit Patterns of Education

Chapter 3 identified at least nine distinct agencies and denominations that are in some way focused on theological education, leadership development, or lay-level discipleship for Inuit communities. These range from non-formal programs to accredited colleges and ordination-track curricula. Most developed out of the same Western approach to education that has characterized K-12 education in the Arctic during the same time period. Recent studies have revealed this system's shortcomings in addressing the educational needs of Inuit K-12 students. Since the church has often relied on the same teaching methods employed in the public classroom, it is obligated to consider these findings and adapt its methods accordingly. Specifically, the anthropological and pedagogical studies of Inuit educational practices surveyed in this chapter reveal four cultural values common across the Arctic Inuit groups that should shape the church's discipleship efforts in these communities.

Sadly, these cultural values did not inform or characterize education in the Inuit Arctic during the twentieth century. Curriculum and educational policy were determined entirely by Western educators, indigenous languages were often forbidden in the classroom, and little consideration was given to what educational strategies might be most effective among the Inuit.[222] The Greenlandic Inuit activist Ingmar Egede, who led Greenland's seminary and teacher training school for many years, summarized his country's situation in 1976:

> Today the Greenlandic school is a product of circumstances that made legislators, educators, and parents disregard the fact that two cultures exist side by side in Greenland. One of the cultures is dominant, because it has defined the political ideology of the development, and has controlled the means of production, the means of communication, the educational institutions, and the administrative machinery. The other culture has been neglected, dying and devalued.[223]

The results of this approach at the K-12 level have been devastating. Graduation rates among indigenous students languish, and those who do graduate tend to perform well-below grade level and find themselves under-prepared for either the workforce or for further education at the post-secondary level.[224] In Canada, the high school graduation rate for Inuit students is estimated at 25-30%.[225] Clifton Bates and Michael Oleksa paint a picture of the legacy of Western education in Alaska, and call for change:

> While some certainly succeed and go on to perform well at the post-secondary level, many, too many, leave school damaged, hurt, wounded, depressed, angry, and tragically suicidal. We believe Alaskans should reflect on what we have been doing for the last hundred years in the name of "education" and consider alternatives.[226]

In recent years, efforts have been made in each Arctic nation to critically evaluate the K-12 education system in order to identify areas for improvement. Many of these findings have been quite specific in nature and apply only to the public K-12 systems in question. Comparatively little research has been done on the related question of adult education at the post-secondary level. An

---

[222] Alaska Natives Commission/Alaska Federation of Natives, "Alaska Native Education: Report of the Education Task Force," in *Alaska Native Education: Views from Within*, eds. Ray Barnhardt & Angayuqaq Oscar Kawagley (Fairbanks: Alaska Native Knowledge Network, 2013). 9-13.
[223] Ingmar Egede, "Educational Problems in Greenland," in *Pedagogik* 6, no. 2 (May 1976). 2.
[224] Alaska Natives Commission, 15-16; Jane P. Preston, Tim R. Claypool, William Rowluck, & Brenda Green, "Exploring the Concepts of Traditional Inuit Leadership and Effective School Leadership in Nunavut (Canada)," *Comparative and International Education* 44.2, article 2 (December 2015), 1.
[225] Heather E. McGregor, *Inuit Education and Schools in the Eastern Arctic* (Vancouver: UBC, 2010). 167.
[226] Clifton Bates & Michael J. Oleksa, *Conflicting Landscapes: American Schooling/Alaska Natives* (Anchorage: Kuskokwim Corporation, 2007). 16.

Alaska Federation of Natives report on education in indigenous communities suggested, "Why some Alaska Native students have difficulty in college can probably be linked to inadequate preparation in high school and to some of the same conditions that make it difficult for them to succeed in high school."[227] Specific factors that this report identifies as contributing to educational success at the K-12 level are teacher turnover, size of student population, poverty and student performance, and the cultural divide.[228]

It is this last factor, the cultural divide, that is most relevant to the current focus on discipleship in the church. The other factors are more systemic in nature and pertain mostly to administrative policy in K-12 schools, but the cultural factor is relevant to education in any context. Elaborating on the cultural divide, the authors of the report observe,

> Native ways of learning are different than traditional Western ways of learning. Much of this is attributable to the high value placed on cooperation by Native culture as opposed to the high value placed on individualism by Western culture. In the words of Mr. John Active, a Yupik who spoke at a University of Alaska Faculty Convocation in 1992, Native students have to become another person, an opposite of their natural selves, to succeed in a traditional American school setting. Traditional Native learning emphasizes quiet observation as opposed to the questioning and active participation emphasized by American-trained educators.[229]

Exploring this divide in more detail, Clifton Bates provides a helpful comparison between the cultural orientation of indigenous students and Western students:

---

[227] Alaska Natives Commission, 22.
[228] Alaska Natives Commission, 16-19.
[229] Alaska Natives Commission, 19.

Table 4.1: Comparison of North American Indigenous and Western Students[230]

North American Indigenous Students	Western Students
Global/holistic	Sequential/linear
Visual/tactile	Auditory
Group good	Individual good
Reflective	Competitive
Learning as a process	Learning as a product
Learning via observation	Learning via verbal explanation & text
Personalism	Professionalism
Skilled in non-verbal communication	Highly verbal
Long wait time	Short wait time
Present	Past-future
External locus of control	Internal locus of control

In comparing anthropological and pedagogical studies on Inuit education in communities across the Arctic, four major cultural values to emerge which can significantly impact the methodology of discipleship: learning through relationship, learning through experience, learning through orality, and learning through the environment. Heather McGregor, in her analysis of traditional Inuit educational values in Nunavut, organizes these under the headings of "Knowing, Being, and Doing," which helpfully correspond with the three dimensions of Christian transformative learning explored in chapter 2, as well as the definition of Ministry Leadership Development established in chapter 1.[231]

Learning through Relationship

Historically, the education of Inuit children was a responsibility of the whole community, and it was personal relationships developed in this context that gave teachers the "right" to instruct. Educators gained the respect and attention of their "students" through warm, caring interpersonal relationships that were established well-before any official educational role was undertaken. In the framework of "knowing, being, and doing," McGregor argues that the relational

---

[230] Adapted from Bates & Oleksa, 134. Bates & Oleksa offer these observations based on their own experiences working with Alaskan students from various indigenous backgrounds. This list does not provide a comprehensive description of Inuit learning styles, but is offered here to illustrate broad differences between Western and North American Indigenous students in general.
[231] McGregor, 46.

component of Inuit education is a function of "being."[232] Education is a function of a person's identity within the community.

The Alaskan writer Fred Savok was an Inupiaq pastor in the Evangelical Covenant Church who lived from 1922-2009. In 2004, he published *Jesus and the Eskimo: How the Man of the Sky Brought the Light to My People.* The book consists of stories relayed to him by his parents, John and Lily Savok, who were children when Westerners first arrived in their region. Savok's memoirs provide valuable first-hand insight to Inuit culture and will provide key data throughout this chapter. He illustrates the importance of relational learning as he describes his mother's enculturation as a child: "when the father left the mother and daughter alone in the cabin, with the morning activities done, they had a woman-to-woman talk about life. Times like these were natural as part of an education for the girl."[233] Education naturally grew out of the parent/child relationship, but it did not end here. Savok shares how after the premature death of his grandfather, his father was taken under the wing of a "kindhearted relative" and educated by the men of the community in the *qasgi*, or the "men's house."[234] Leona Okakok summarizes the importance of these community relationships in the education process:

> In the traditional Iñupiat Eskimo culture, education was everybody's business. It was okay to admonish, scold, or otherwise correct the behavior of any child, whether or not one was a relative. The success of the child's education depended in large part on how well his or her parents accepted admonishment of their child by other members of their own community. We as a people valued this acceptance highly because we knew that every member of our village was involved in some way with equipping our child for success.[235]

The Inuuqatigiit Curriculum developed in 1995 for and by the Inuit region of the Northwest Territories (now Nunavut) makes the same affirmation: "Children were educated by the people around them. Various family members accepted responsibility for different aspects of children's education."[236] In Greenland, Egede highlighted the importance of these relationships in the education process:

---

[232] McGregor, 48.
[233] Fred Savok, *Jesus and the Eskimo: How the Man of the Sky Brought the Light to My People* (Fairbanks: HLC, 2004). 157.
[234] Savok, 102, 154.
[235] Leona Okakok, "Serving the Purpose of Education," in *Alaska Native Education: Views from Within* (Fairbanks: Alaska Native Knowledge Network, 2013). 108-109.
[236] Department of Education, Culture, and Employment; *Inuuqatigiit: The Curriculum from the Inuit Perspective* (Yellowknife: Northwest Territories, 1996). 15.

While growing up, the children were in constant contact with the grown-ups in the family. Apart from the children and the parents, the grandparents often lived in the house, too; and frequently there was also an aunt or an uncle, who had not married yet. It is difficult to distinguish between play and training for adulthood.[237]

Across the arctic, education was a community affair grounded in personal relationship.

Twentieth-century pedagogical studies confirm the importance of this relational dynamic. In her study of student/teacher dynamics in Alaska Native high schools, Judith Kleinfeld observes,

Village students tend to desire highly personalized relationships not only with their classmates, but also with their teachers. Thus, village students generally desire teachers to be friends in the full sense of the term, while teachers generally desire village students to be only students. The yearning of students [is] to become personal friends with their teachers and to resolve academic problems in a social, not a task-oriented situation...[238]

Comparing this expectation with the four major teaching styles that she observes, Kleinfeld concludes,

The essence of the instructional style that elicits a high level of intellectual performance from village Indian and Eskimo students is to create an extremely warm personal relationship and, within it, to actively demand a high level of academic work. Village students thus interpret the teacher's demandingness not as bossiness or hostility, but rather as an expression of his personal concern. Meeting the teacher's academic standards becomes their reciprocal obligation in an intensely personal relationship.[239]

Kleinfeld makes an important distinction between what she labels "Sentimentalists"—warm, friendly teachers who have difficulty placing any real demands upon their students—and "Supportive Gadflies," who use their strong personal relationship as a motivator to encourage academic achievement.[240] Little learning takes place under the former type, but Inuit students respond very positively to the personal-yet-demanding approach of Supportive Gadfly teachers. When a strong relationship is in place, students interpret the academic demands "as an aspect of the teacher's personal concern for the

---

[237] Egede, 3.
[238] Judith Kleinfeld, *Effective Teachers of Indian and Eskimo High School Students* (Fairbanks: Institute of Social, Economic and Government Research, 1972). 11.
[239] Kleinfeld, *Effective Teachers*, 41.
[240] Kleinfeld, *Effective Teachers*, 33-35.

student, rather than as concern for subject matter."[241] Essentially, students receive instruction from this type of teacher much as they would interpret instruction from a parent, a relative, or a community elder.

Kleinfeld's research suggests that learning through relationship is a crucial value to acknowledge and cultivate in the discipleship process, though it is very much at odds with the traditional Western approach. Kleinfeld observes,

> Many teachers, especially upper-grade teachers, have been socialized by their university training and professional associations to regard impersonal professionalism as the appropriate mode of relating to students.[242]

This is certainly true of the traditional seminary environment, which emphasizes a highpower distance between faculty and students and minimal interpersonal interaction outside the classroom. Kleinfeld finds that rural Alaskan students generally interpret such professional distance as disinterest or hostility.[243] Conversely, "The intense personal warmth that seems to lead to effective teaching of village Indian and Eskimo students often appears inappropriate to Western professionals."[244]

Learning through Experience

The second educational value observed in traditional Inuit culture is that of learning through experience—in other words, *doing*: "Observation, practise, and experience were the most common and favoured methods of facilitating skills and knowledge acquisition."[245] Again, Savok provides insight from his family's experience, this time focusing on how his aunt, Keenaq, learned the skill of leatherwork:

> Qutuq was a good mother-teacher to her children. Keenaq, her daughter, sometimes would be fascinated watching her mother cut skins for garments. Most of the time the skin sewer never bothered to measure before cutting. Serious eye-sighting usually brought good results. But, once in a while, she would use her hand and fingers as measuring tools. Her education in the trade of skin-sewing was heightened by viewing the finished garments her mother made. It would not be long before Keenaq herself would be displaying finished garments of skin for others to enjoy. Right now, she enjoyed learning by watching. But the stories of life, of how things were done, and what material they were made of, her mother would tell as she kept her needle and thread going deftly with her practiced fingers, were

---

[241] Kleinfeld, *Effective Teachers*, 1.
[242] Kleinfeld, *Effective Teachers*, 17.
[243] Kleinfeld, *Effective Teachers*, 20.
[244] Kleinfeld, *Effective Teachers*, 5.
[245] McGregor, 46.

interesting. Now and then, the mother-teacher would take time and explain the correct use of different garment materials and what kind of sinew to use for a specific garment. These were important against wear-and-tear of different clothing needed by the family.[246]

Education is traditionally a hands-on experience in the Inuit culture. In many communities, written instruction has only been introduced in the last 100 years, and even verbal instruction is kept to a minimum. Rather, people learn primarily by watching and doing:

> Fishing, hunting, and food gathering and preparation practices are passed on to children by working with, observing, and mimicking their parents, grandparents, and older siblings. Typically, the person teaching the skill will say very little. The learner is expected to observe closely and mimic what is being done. It is quite common for children to become quite skillful with a variety of tools, including sharp knives, at an early age.[247]

The *Inuuqatigiit* curriculum in Canada affirms the same principle:

> Children were encouraged to practice and learn with all their senses. It made them aware that learning involves the whole body. With repetition, practice, and progression, the instruction built their confidence, giving them a sense of accomplishment and pride in their abilities. Eventually, the child was able to do the whole task from beginning to end.[248]

Summarizing the same experiential value among the Greenlandic Inuit, Egede wrote, "It is difficult to distinguish between play and training for adulthood. By taking part in the daily life of the family, the children learned the necessary skills as they gradually developed the ability to master them."[249]

These cultural observations are supported by formal pedagogical research. In his survey of research in this field, Arthur More concluded that Inuit students tested very highly in perceptual, spatial, and mechanical processing and

---

[246] Savok, 102.
[247] Angayuqaq Oscar Kawagaley, Delena Norris-Tull, & Roger Norris-Tull, "The Indigenous Worldview of Yupiaq Culture: Its Scientific Nature and Relevance to the Practice and Teaching of Science," in *Alaska Native Education: Views from Within* (Fairbanks: Alaska Native Knowledge Network, 2010). 225-226.
[248] NT Department of Education, Culture, and Employment, 14.
[249] Egede, 3.

imaginal coding; and comparatively weakly in verbal coding.[250] Kleinfeld's research led to similar conclusions.[251]

Bates and Oleksa compare this orientation to the traditional Western approach to learning, which focuses primarily on lecture and reading:

> The Eskimos are of a culture and environment where there is little experience with the purpose of literacy and little exposure to reading and writing behavior, linguistic concepts or language usage. The education system must take this into consideration... Along with this is the cultural trait of emphasizing learning via observation, not by verbal explanations... These skills, though, are not valued by the standard western school system. The system concentrates on verbal ability and, for the most part, the transfer of abstract information to students via lecture and text.[252]

They go on to propose greater emphasis upon spatial ability and perceptual skills in the K-12 curriculum within Inuit communities, listing examples such as "mapping, geometry, mechanics, drawing, carving, and model building."[253] Kawagaley, et al., provide insightful application of this principle to contemporary pedagogical theory:

> To translate Yupiaq teaching and learning into current educational jargon, one could state that teaching strongly emphasizes modeling and guided practice, and that cooperative learning, peer tutoring, and hands-on learning are essential strategies.[254]

Learning through the Environment

A third traditional value that is frequently emphasized in discussions of Inuit education is the importance of the environment. This is a natural outgrowth of the Inuit worldview, which sees humans and the natural world existing in close relationship.[255] Inuit survival depended on correctly understanding and adapting to the world around them:

> It is through direct interaction with the environment that the Yupiaq people learn... As the Yupiaq people interact with nature, they carefully observe to find pattern or order where there might otherwise appear to be chaos. The

---

[250] Arthur J. More, "Learning Styles and Indian Students: A Review of Research," paper presented at the Mokakit Indian Education Research Conference (London, Ontario, Canada, July 25-27, 1984). 7-10.
[251] Judith Kleinfeld, "Intellectual Strengths in Culturally Different Groups: An Eskimo Illustration," *Review of Educational Research* 43, no. 3 (September 1973), 341-359.
[252] Bates & Oleksa, 136-138.
[253] Bates & Oleska, 175.
[254] Kawagaley, Norris-Tull, & Norris-Tull, 226.
[255] Kawagaley, 86-87.

> Yupiaq people's empirical knowledge of their environment has to be general and specific at the same time. During their hunting trips into the tundra or on the ocean in the winter, they must have precise knowledge of the snow and ice conditions, so over many years of experience and observation they have classified snow and ice with terms having very specific meanings. For example, there are at least 37 Yupiat terms for ice, having to do with seasons, weather conditions, solar energy transformations, currents, and rapid changes in wind direction and velocity. To the Yupiaq people, it is a matter of survival.[256]

McGregor interprets this educational value as a function of *knowing*: "As a result of the constraints placed on the Inuit by the Arctic ecosystem, their daily pursuits demanded a high level of environmental knowledge."[257]

John Collier explores this traditional perspective and compares it to the Western approach:

> Traditional Eskimo learning was fundamentally a training in observation and the analysis of this sensory reception. Content was frequently nonverbal and ecological in experience—weather prediction, ice prediction, warnings of blizzards, the drift of game. White learning shifted attention to the verbal and the literate, which had survival value in abstract circumstances usually unrelated to the natural world surrounding the school.[258]

In contemporary pedagogy, this value tends to be applied most notably in the field of science education. "Native ways of knowing" has become a common theme in discussions of STEM education in Alaska, as Western scientists continue to find that the hallowed scientific method often affirms cultural knowledge about the environment that has been passed down orally for generations.[259] In Canada, the same theme is denoted by *Inuit Qaujimajatuqangit* ("IQ"), paraphrased by McGregor as "Inuit ways of knowing, being, and doing."[260] In response, science teachers in the public school system are encouraged to incorporate study of the local environment into their curricula, paying careful attention to integration of the scientific method and

---

[256] Kawagaley, 88-89.
[257] McGregor, 44.
[258] John Collier, Jr., *Alaskan Eskimo Education: A film Analysis of Cultural Confrontation in the Schools* (San Francisco: Holt, Rinehart, & Winston, 1973). 39.
[259] Patricia A. L. Conchran, Catherine A. Marshall, Carmen Garcia-Downing, Elizabeth Kendall, Doris Cook, Laurie McCubbin, & Reva Mariah S. Gover, "Indigenous Ways of Knowing: Implications for Participatory Research and Community," in *American Journal of Public Health*, vol. 98, no. 1 (January 2008), 22-27.
[260] McGregor, 34.

cultural knowledge.[261] For example, Standard B for educators in the *Alaska Standards for Culturally Responsive Schools* reads, "Culturally-responsive educators use the local environment and community resources on a regular basis to link what they are teaching to the everyday lives of the students."[262]

Learning through Orality

The value of experience as discussed earlier does not exclude the spoken word, and forms of lecture must certainly find their place in a contextualized Inuit discipleship curriculum. This is evidenced through the strong emphasis placed on orality in many accounts of traditional Inuit educational practices. This connection between experience and spoken instruction leads McGregor to group the values of experience and orality together under the heading of "doing." That said, orality might just as easily fit under the category of "knowing," since it serves as the primary means of information transfer between teacher and learner. Of course, one might also argue that orality is a function of "being," since the identity of the teacher, the learner, and the entire community is stored, expressed, and transmitted through the oral tradition.[263] It is perhaps best not to force "orality" into one of the three constituent components of transformative learning, but rather to see it as a vehicle or agent that facilitates transformation in all three domains.

Relational learning, environmental learning, and experiential learning comprise the three philosophical "pillars" of Inuit education, corresponding to the ontological, epistemological, and methodological categories of "being," "knowing," and "doing." Orality describes *how* these three "pillars" are erected in each successive generation. To use a different metaphor, if the community, the environment, and experience are three runners on a sled, then orality is the engine (or the dog team) that moves it forward.

Once again, Fred Savok's memoirs illustrate this value:

> "Son, don't neglect to go to the qasgi [men's hall] and listen to hunting stories. It is important for you to hear and learn of hunting..." mother told her son. As much as Qutuq would love to teach her son she, as a woman, was unable to teach the why's and how's of hunting. The best she could do was to encourage young Savok to join other boys in the qasgi and learn.[264]

Notice the emphasis on "hunting stories"—not "hunting lessons" or "hunting presentations." Inuit boys and girls did not learn the details of the subsistence

---

[261] Ray Barnhardt & Angayuqaq Oscar Kawagley, "Culture, Chaos, and Complexity," in *Alaska Native Education: Views from Within* (Fairbanks: Alaska Native Knowledge Network, 2010). 211.
[262] Assembly of Alaska Native Educators, *Alaska Standards for Culturally-Responsive Schools* (Fairbanks: Alaska Native Knowledge Network, 1998). 10.
[263] Matthews, 86-87.
[264] Savok, 102.

lifestyle through a how-to manual or a step-by-step curriculum. Across the Arctic, this knowledge was passed down from generation to generation orally, in story form.[265]

> There were no libraries or computers in the past. The important things that needed to be passed down were in the stories and songs that everyone heard. Everything was in the mind and each person was responsible for learning the lessons of previous generations… In order for this exchange to take place there needs to be a time and place for Elders to express themselves.[266]

This was true not only of the Alaskan Inuit, but in Canada as well, as demonstrated by this account from the Inuvialuit Inuit of Western Canada:

> In the time before the Inuvialuit had books, our elders, both men and women, were the keepers of Inuvialuit knowledge. Without them, each generation would have had to have learned everything there was to know by discovering it themselves. The elders also had the wisdom of age and experience. Anybody wanting to learn had only to sit and listen to an elder speak. The hunters especially relied heavily upon the stories and advice given by their elders so they could become better hunters and leaders.[267]

In the same way, Egede emphasizes the importance of the oral tradition in Greenlandic education:

> During the evenings and the periods of bad weather, when the men were at home, they spent their time making or repairing their hunting tools. On these occasions the hunters told about their confrontations with weather, ice, sea, and especially with the game… Through the tales the hunters shared each others' experiences, and the boys were introduced to the kind of life that lay ahead of them.[268]

This evidence counters an assumption that might otherwise arise out of the experiential emphasis observed earlier—that there is little room for informational content in contextualized Inuit education, and that all learning is simply a matter of personal demonstration followed by hands-on trial and error. Lucy Jones-Sparck describes how impactful this mode of education could be in the correct context:

---

[265] NT Department of Education, Culture, and Employment, 19.
[266] Carl Hild, "Alaska Native Traditional Knowledge and Ways of Knowing," in *Alaska Native Education: Views from Within* (Fairbanks: Alaska Native Knowledge Network, 2010). 164.
[267] NT Department of Education, Culture, and Employment, 46.
[268] Egede, 4.

From the accounts of the Cup'ik Elders today, a more intense atmosphere of learning existed in the *qaygiq* (men's house). In the active listening times when an Elder was lecturing, the men reported that they found it difficult to clear their throats or even to scratch an itch on their bodies. This resulted from the high esteem they had for Elders, which bordered on fear.[269]

Indeed, though hands-on learning is indispensable to Inuit learning styles, the importance of this oral tradition emphasizes that there is a time and place for the "sage on the stage" who transmits knowledge orally.

From a contemporary pedagogical perspective, K-12 literacy scores in Inuit communities continue to lag behind national norms. Clifton Bates argues convincingly that the solution is not simply to emphasize more reading in the curriculum, but to intentionally place more emphasis oral language proficiency.[270] Again, this is not to suggest that reading should be eliminated from the curriculum, but simply that educators should begin from a point of strength in order to encourage more effective learning. Greater oral proficiency in what Bates calls "school language," in turn, provides a stronger foundation for literacy skills.[271] Oleksa and Dauenhauer demonstrate how the Russian Orthodox school system of the 1800s was able to produce many highly-literate and successful Aleut leaders precisely because it "attempted to build on indigenous talent and potential, and channel it to new fulfillment in new directions, such as literacy."[272] This is opposed to the Western system that supplanted the Russian Orthodox schools in the 1900s, taking an assimilationist approach that imposed English-language curriculum and European educational philosophy.

Inuit Patterns of Leadership

Having developed a general regionalized portrayal of Inuit cultural values pertaining to education, attention now turns to Inuit leadership patterns. If the goal is to develop Inuit ministry leaders, then a contextualized understanding of Inuit leadership is essential. An ethnographic survey of circumpolar Inuit cultures reveals four key values pertaining to leadership that are common to communities across the region: informality, age, character, and knowledge.

---

[269] Lucy Jones-Sparck, "Effects of Modernization on the Cup'ik of Alaska," in *Alaska Native Education: Views from Within* (Fairbanks: Alaska Native Knowledge Network, 2010). 319.
[270] Bates & Oleksa, 170-171.
[271] Bates & Oleksa, 177.
[272] Michael Oleksa & Richard Dauenhauer, "Education in Russian America," in *Education in Alaska's Past* (Anchorage: Alaska Historical Society, 1982). 56.

Informality

Informality is perhaps the defining value of leadership in Inuit society. Anthropologist Steve Langdon summarizes the traditional stereotype: "Eskimo society has long been considered a model of egalitarianism in which all men were equal and judged solely by their achievements."[273] However, he is quick to qualify this generalization. Leadership was important to Inuit society; it was simply not expressed through centralized and hierarchical positions of power. Traditional Inuit society revolved around kinship relationships, with most communities consisting of related individuals connected by bilateral family ties.[274] The group would collaborate for mutual survival in a harsh environment, engaging in subsistence activities such as whaling and caribou hunting that could not be undertaken by a single individual.

Day-to-day life in Inuit society was very much a partnership between equals. Mathiassen describes that among the Greenlandic Inuit,

> There was no real organization above the family, no clans, no tribes, no chiefs. At each settlement there was usually an older, experienced man, who "thought" for the settlement and whose advice was generally followed, although there was no obligation to do so.[275]

Norman Chance observed that among the Inupiat, "Since there was no political organization, social sanctions, customary law, common goals, and norms provided the essential fabric of village structure. The individual had great freedom of choice in his actions, but his security lay in cooperating and sharing with others."[276] Similarly, among the Yupiit,

> there existed a strong ethos of egalitarian, community-focused ideology in which elders as a collective were seen as a critical resource for the welfare of all... While leaders coordinated the construction and use of the qasigih, accumulated and distributed wealth, those activities did not result in hereditary statuses.[277]

No individual had authority over the whole group, and decisions were made collectively through consensus.

Since the advent of Western society and political organization, the form of leadership has changed somewhat, though the values remain. Kinship ties are

---

[273] Langdon, 75.
[274] Langdon, 57, 73.
[275] Therkel Mathiassen, "Ethnology of the Greenland Eskimos," in *Encylopedia Arctica*, vol. 8 (Washington: Office of Naval Research, 1951). 16.
[276] Norman Chance, *The Eskimo of North Alaska* (New York: Holt, Rinehart, and Winston, 1966), 65.
[277] Langdon, 57-58.

deemphasized, and communities today consist of many different families. Ridley notes, "The village is now the focus of leadership outside the immediate family... The underlying values of leadership continue, though new forms and additional factors are present."[278] So though the kinship-based leadership structure has essentially been replaced by the village council, the same informal approach is valued and expected. An effective leader is not one who aspires to the role and exercises authority, but rather one who is recognized by the community and acts as spokesman, mediator, and consensus-builder. These same leadership values apply not only at the local level, but also within the post-ANCSA Native Corporations in Alaska, provincial-level leadership in Canadian Nunavut, and national-level leadership under Greenlandic home-rule.

Age/Experience

If informality describes the manner of leadership in Inuit society, then age might be the most obvious descriptor of Inuit leaders themselves. It was primarily through hunting activities that leadership roles were exercised. Egede saw age and experience as intrinsically related aspects of leadership in Greenland:

> In the static community, experience and age were important to a degree, which is about to be forgotten in a dynamic community. The older one grew, the more variations one had seen of the pattern which is followed by the different years and the lives of the individuals.[279]

The Inuvialuit of northwestern Canada recount, "The best hunters became our leaders. A hunter became a leader only by proving himself over a long period of time."[280] Among the Inuvialuit as well as the Inupiat of northern Alaska, the *umialik*, or "he who has a boat," provided important leadership for the community.[281] This role was "responsible for many activities including the whale hunt, the qargi, ceremonies, festivals, religious rituals and trading expeditions."[282] The Yupiit of Western Alaska were generally not whalers, but a similar role is evidenced in the *nukalpiak*, or "good hunter"—"Not only did he contribute wood for the communal fire bath and oil to keep the lamps lit, but he also figured prominently in midwinter ceremonial distributions."[283] Ann Fienup-Riordan provides a helpful distinction between these two leadership roles:

---

[278] Ridley, 78-79.
[279] Egede, 4.
[280] NT Department of Education, Culture, and Employment; 74.
[281] NT Department of Education, Culture, and Employment; 74.
[282] Langdon, 75.
[283] Ann Fienup-Riordan, *Qaluyaarmiuni Nunamtenek Qanemciput: Our Nelson Island Stories* (Anchorage: Calista Elders Council, 2011), xvi.

The position of the *nukalpiaq* was not, however, comparable to that of the *umialik*, or whaling captain of northern Alaska, who had the power to collect the surplus and much of the basic production of individual family members and redistribute it. Instead, the less centralized system in western Alaska had every local extended family vying with the others in their ability to gather and redistribute surplus during both informal and ritual redistribution.[284]

So both the *umialik* and *nukalpiaq* emerged out of a similar subsistence context focused on providing for the community. Though the *umialik* exerted a greater degree of influence and oversight than the *nukalpiaq*, neither functioned as a hierarchical or authoritarian leader. Both roles were ascribed by the community through mutual recognition and respect rather than being inherited or achieved through personal ambition. Importantly, neither was an exclusive position—there would often be several to a community.[285] These roles of were not generally given to younger hunters and whalers, since multiple seasons of successful hunting were prerequisite for the positions.

Ridley consistently emphasizes that the leaders were older men who had demonstrated ability.[286] This leads to a third leadership role that is universally respected and honored throughout Inuit society—the village "elders." As Fienup-Riordan notes, "Although the prowess and generosity of the *nukalpiaq* was a primary focus of both political and economic integration, the counsel and valued knowledge of elders, who not only advised when to harvest but when distribution was appropriate, mitigated his authority."[287] Since leadership was traditionally kinship-based, it was naturally the older generation that provided leadership and guidance for the young.[288] Nevertheless, age in itself does not define leadership among the Inuit, as not all elders exert an equal degree of influence. Rather, it is the experience, wisdom, and resources gained through age that gives influence in the community.[289] As Ridley observes, "The environmental challenges require the direction of accumulated knowledge and experience of the elders."[290]

---

[284] Ann Fienup-Riordan, *Boundaries and Passages: Rule and Ritual in Yup'ik Eskimo Oral Tradition* (Norman: University of Oklahoma, 1994), 37.
[285] Ridley, 60, 64.
[286] Ridley, 75.
[287] Fienup-Riordan, *Boundaries and Passages*, 37.
[288] Chance, 62.
[289] NT Department of Education, Culture, and Employment, 47.
[290] Ridley, 59.

Character

A third common Inuit cultural value pertaining to leadership is that of character. Ridley identifies several ideal character qualities of an Inuit leader: "good judgment, industriousness and generosity."[291] It was the strength of a person's character—as defined by community expectations—that gave influence in the group, and "authority came from their prestige as examples of cultural ideals."[292] In short, an Inuit leader is a person that the community has observed and determined to be worth following. Most often, generosity is the trait that is mentioned as desirable in a leader. The role of the *umialik* and to a lesser extent the *nukalpiaq* in sharing and distributing food has already been noted. In this harsh climate, provision of food was of paramount importance, and a generous person was a person worth following. Langdon describes what was expected of the *umialik* in this regard:

> Each of six- to eight-man crews independently pursued whales and competed to be the first to strike one. A complex distributional formula awarded the first captain and crew a majority of the whale but the second through eighth crews who came to their assistance all received portions. The first captain and his wife then held a feast for the entire village. Thus competition, cooperation and sharing were elegantly united in joint communal activities that made possible sizable, sustainable Inupiat communities.[293]

The priority of generosity suggests that wealthier individuals would be more readily accepted as leaders. However, in traditional Yup'ik economy, hunting provided the only source of personal "income," so again it was the successful hunters who would have a surplus to share.[294] Among the Inupiat, whaling requires a greater amount of resources: "As well as skill and a willingness to work hard, a modern whaling captain must have the economic capital to purchase all necessary equipment and supplies."[295] For this reason, Langdon notes that though the role was open to anyone, "those who inherited whaling equipment and training had a head start in attaining *umialik* status."[296]

The core issue behind the need for generosity is character. A person is not required to be rich in order to be a leader, but those with resources—whether it be special training, skill, or material wealth—are expected to use it for the

---

[291] Ridley, 59.
[292] Ridley, 65.
[293] Langdon, 68.
[294] Margaret Lantis, *The Social Culture of the Nunivak Eskimo* (Philadelphia: American Philosophical Society, 1946), 247.
[295] Chance, 40.
[296] Langdon, 75.

good of the community. Only after establishing a track record of admirable character that portrays the community's ideals does an individual earn influence in the community.

Knowledge

Knowledge is often gained through age and experience, and an Inuit leader is expected to be knowledgeable in order to benefit the community. The importance of knowing the best hunting techniques and locations has already been discussed as it relates to the *nukalpiaq* and *umialik*, and no one could achieve these roles without having mastered the annual subsistence cycle. In the same way, the elders are expected to pass on their knowledge to the younger generations through oral tradition.[297] Laugrand & Oosten emphasize that in Nunavut, "Age was always an important factor in the distribution of knowledge. Knowledge was precious; it was not shared with everyone, but was only passed on to close relatives or sold at a good price."[298]

The importance of knowledge leads to a fourth and final leadership role that was important in ancient times—that of the shaman. Norman Chance sees the shaman as "the most dominant aboriginal leader... since his influence consistently extended beyond the kin group to the village at large."[299] In his survey of shamanism across the circumpolar Inuit groups from Siberia to Greenland, Erik Holtved concluded that "the position and traditional functions of the shaman in general have had a rather uniform stamp all over this vast area."[300] Shamans were leaders primarily within the all-important spiritual sphere, which encompassed the totality of life for the Inuit. Their ability to communicate with, manipulate, and appease the spirits meant that shamans were powerful leaders that transcended kinship ties:

> Even so, animal and human spirits wandered the earth, as did monsters and creatures of the deep and the underground, good spirits and evil spirits (*alangrut*) that either helped or caused havoc, even death, for humans and animals alike. Every physical manifestation—plenty of food or famine, good weather or bad, good luck or bad, health or illness—had a spiritual cause. This is why the shamans, the *angalkuq*, were the most important men and women in the village.[301]

---

[297] Fienup-Riordan, *Boundaries and Passages*, 37.
[298] Laugrand & Oosten, 18.
[299] Chance, 62.
[300] Holtved, Erik, "Eskimo Shamanism," in *Scripta Instituti Donneriani Aboensis*, vol. 1 (August 1967). 23-31. 23.
[301] Napoleon, 8.

It was precisely this "special knowledge which the group at large did not share" that afforded the shaman a position of leadership in the community.[302]

In contemporary society, the shaman is no more.[303] In the rapid Westernization that took place during the early twentieth century, Inuit communities across the arctic turned away from shamanism through an odd combination of Christian missionary work, Western secularization, and government oppression. In the message of Christ, the Inuit found a greater spiritual power than that offered by the shamans.[304] In Western medicine and technology, they found better cures for disease and tools for hunting.[305] And through active oppression by the colonial governments in Alaska and Canada, which mandated educational policies that forbade expressions of indigenous language and culture, knowledge of the "old ways" of the shaman faded out of existence.[306]

That said, the value of knowledge—most often environmental and spiritual—continues to be important to leadership in Inuit communities today. Moreover, the "niche" that the shaman once filled continues to exist, and has today been filled by another office:

> Missionaries—along with teachers and medical professionals—took for themselves much of the social function once performed by the shamans... The missionaries knew of the supernatural, set about contacting it, and did so on behalf of those in trouble. In this the "supershaman" helped them; the "chief of spirits" was their helping spirit.[307]

Perhaps more reflective of good missiological strategy (and the ultimate vision of this present study), Norman Chance observes that the contemporary indigenous lay minister also fills this niche.[308]

Inuit Patterns of Social Control

A final cultural dynamic that must be considered in the process of indigenous leadership development is that of social control. Social control is intrinsic to the leadership development process, since it must be exercised by

---

[302] Ridley, 61, 65.
[303] Napoleon, 11.
[304] Dorothy Jean Ray, *The Eskimos of Bering Strait, 1650-1898* (Seattle: University of Washington, 1975), 251.
[305] Chance, 2-3.
[306] Napoleon, 13.
[307] Larry Jorgenson, "From Shamans to Missionaries: The Popular Religiosity of the Inupiaq Eskimo," *Word & World*, vol. 10, no. 4, 339-348, 345-346.
[308] Chance, 63.

educators as they supervise the teaching/learning process, as well as by ministry leaders themselves as they shepherd their communities of faith.

Considering once again the three approaches to social control as defined in chapter 2, the Inuit cultures would seem to fit most naturally into "Fear/Power" orientation. Muller and Georges both identify fear of the supernatural as a fundamental characteristic of animistic cultures and "tribal" societies, which would presumably include the Inuit.[309] Nevertheless, the educational studies surveyed above, coupled with my (John's) six years of personal experience teaching Inuit students, suggest that this traditional focus on the supernatural dimension does not accurately represent the "heart" of contemporary Inuit culture. The "spirit world" of their ancestors is rarely a major motivator in the day-to-day actions of Inuit students today. That said, it is clear that the usual Western approaches are equally ineffective as motivators. I (John) remember quite clearly when a student abruptly left my office mid-conversation after I communicated a bit too bluntly regarding some poor academic decisions. Though I attempted to provide personal motivation by appealing to the individual sense of reward and punishment, the student simply perceived accusations against their character, and chose to save face by leaving the room. As educators, and even more importantly as ministers, it is crucial to understand the historic and contemporary orientations of the culture. Inuit approaches to such issues have not remained static over the years, nor have they simply adopted the individualistic Western framework oriented around personal guilt and innocence. Diachronic study of Inuit culture suggests that the influence of Western secularization has caused a shift from a predominantly Fear/Power orientation towards social control to a greater emphasis on Honor/Shame.

The lack of written history in Inuit culture prior to European contact complicates this task of diachronic anthropology but does not render it impossible. Although there exist no written accounts of the culture from an insider perspective, two types of material do exist that enable the present study: first-hand oral accounts that have been passed down generationally, and second-hand observations made by early Western anthropologists.

"The Old Ways": Social Control through Fear & Power

Fred Savok's parents, John and Lily Savok, were children when Westerners first arrived in their region. John and Lily's parents were some of the first Alaskan Inuit to convert to faith in Jesus. Savok's work is quite insightful to the discussion at hand, since his stories span at least four generations, providing first-hand insight not only to the ancient role of the shaman in his Inuit culture, but also to how the message of the gospel was first understood by the Inupiat.

---

[309] Muller, 43; Georges, 11.

The themes of fear and power permeate Savok's writing. His story begins in the days of his grandparents, prior to European arrival. Of these days, he writes:

> Prior to the coming of the belief in Christianity and the importance of Jesus, Eskimo culture was under the influence of the Anatkut (Shaman). Some Anatkut believed they received their power from above, while others got their power from the darkness, from below. These Anatkut had power over the people because they were the keepers of the taboos. The taboos were never to be broken otherwise people would suffer the consequences, even to death.[310]

This fear was not a distant theoretical concept for Savok's family, but was central to their identity and personal experience. He shares how his maternal grandmother, Qutleruq, became all too acquainted with the violation of supernatural taboo at a young age. Qutleruq's father had recently become seriously ill. The shaman was invited to the home, where he performed a ritual that resulted in healing several days later. However, the healing came with a strict warning from the shaman: no one in the family was to make any sort of braid, or the father would die immediately. Several weeks later, as she was playing with her friends, Qutleruq noticed a commotion in the village nearby:

> The poor girl did not need to be told. She knew what happened. She had killed her father by braiding grass. The half-finished work of grass fell slowly down from her hands to the sand below. She froze with fear, looking toward the *qasgi* [men's hall]. Slowly and fearfully, Qutleruq started walking toward the *qasgi*. She felt so weak from fear that she could not run.[311]

The emphasis on fear in his grandmother's story must be noted. Summarizing the entire ethos of the day, Savok writes, "So the poor Eskimo lived in constant fear. Fear of death seemed to lurk just outside the door of each humble home."[312]

In addition to the piercing account summarized above, Savok identifies many other ritual taboos through the stories that he tells. Women must isolate themselves from the community for several days during childbirth, and in the event of stillbirth, all clothing must be burned.[313] A baby could be caught in a dipnet upon delivery as a good omen to provide physical strength.[314] Eating unripened salmonberries would cause a person to die in sleep that night, and

---

[310] Savok, 12.
[311] Savok, 20.
[312] Savok, 19.
[313] Savok, 31.
[314] Savok, 32.

"seeing the eggs in the nest of a certain snipe would certainly cause a relative to die."[315] Functionalist anthropologists could presumably identify reasons for each of these taboos, as will be duly noted shortly, but for the present time, it is important to let the oral history speak for itself. As Savok summarizes, "To an average Eskimo's life situation, fear permeated his whole life to the core."[316]

A person might, at this point, take issue with Savok's portrayal, noting his occupation as a Christian pastor and his own semi-acculturated perspective. Would this not certainly taint his understanding of his ancestors' experiences? It is necessary here to meet Savok on his own terms. He emphasizes the importance of the oral tradition that he is passing on and his own loyalty to represent this history accurately:

> Since the Eskimo did not have a written history to pass on from generation to generation, their ability to retain information was fantastic. Retelling a long story exactly as told, after hearing it only once, was not hard for many… And I have prayerfully decided to portray these true-to-life happenings as best as I know how in story form. Undoubtedly, some segments of truth and activities will differ from other Native authors. Although the basic truths about Eskimo culture are the same, how we express those stories in a difficult language of English is the blame for sure.[317]

The discussion now briefly turns to another of these Native authors that Savok acknowledges.

The writings of Harold Napoleon, a Yup'ik author who provides prophetic critique of his own cultural heritage from a more sociological perspective, demonstrate much the same "fear/power" orientation that emerges from Savok's portrayal. Napoleon uses the Yup'ik word *yuuyaraq* to describe the "old ways," which he translates as "the way of being a human being."[318] This unwritten law, he writes, "outlined the protocol for every and any situation that human beings might find themselves in… It outlined the way of living in harmony within this spirit world and with the spirit beings that inhabited this world."[319] Expanding on this spirit world and the principle of *yuuyaraq*, Napoleon echoes many of the same themes that arose in Savok's work:

> Even so, animal and human spirits wandered the earth, as did monsters and creatures of the deep and the underground, good spirits and evil spirits (*alangrut*) that either helped or caused havoc, even death, for humans and animals alike. Every physical manifestation—plenty of food or famine, good

---

[315] Savok, 108.
[316] Savok, 41.
[317] Savok, 13-15.
[318] Napoleon, 4.
[319] Napoleon, 5.

weather or bad, good luck or bad, health or illness—had a spiritual cause. This is why the shamans, the *angalkuq*, were the most important men and women in the village.[320]

Notably, though Napoleon avoids the emphasis on fear that pervaded Savok's portrayal, the theme of power is just as evident. Correct behavior for the Yup'ik, like the Inupiat, focused on appeasing the spirits and gaining power.

Looking back on the "old ways," contemporary anthropologists have tended to agree with this assessment. Placing these oral traditions within the functionalist framework that has tended to dominate Western anthropology, the dynamics of fear and power are understood as elements of social control. Steve Langdon, for example, describes taboos similar to those acknowledged by Savok and Napoleon:

> Women were trained in the skills of tanning, sewing and food preparation; wives observed many taboos and rituals to assist their husbands' hunting. These included a broad range of activities such as cutting skins at certain times, eating certain foods or looking in certain directions. It was thought that if those taboos were broken, then bad luck would befall the husband's hunting efforts.[321]

Similar taboos relating to hunting, childbirth, and healing have been documented by the Canadian Inuit.[322] Norman Chance theorizes about the anthropological "function" behind these religious beliefs, suggesting they could "be called upon to 'explain' a temporary loss of food supply: a kin member had broken an important taboo or an evil spirit had driven away the game."[323] Chance elaborates further on the role of power in ancient Inupiat society:

> Essentially, the Eskimo perception of the universe was one of internal harmony of the elements in which various natural and supernatural forces were neutrally disposed toward man. By means of ritual and magic, however, the Eskimo could influence the supernatural forces toward a desired end, be it controlling the weather and food supply, ensuring protection against illness, or curing illness when it struck. The power to influence these events came from the use of charms, amulets, and magical formulas, observance of taboos, and the practice of sorcery.[324]

---

[320] Napoleon, 8.
[321] Steve J. Langdon, *The Native People of Alaska: Traditional Living in a Northern Land* (Anchorage: Greatland, 2002), 75.
[322] NT Department of Education, Culture, and Employment; 51, 55, 70.
[323] Norman Chance, *The Eskimo of North Alaska* (New York: Holt, Rinehart, and Winston, 1966), 2.
[324] Chance, 58.

These anthropological perspectives help affirm what has been inferred from the accounts of the cultural insiders, Savok and Napoleon. Working from a functionalist framework, they propose that the supernatural perspective served to help the Inuit make sense of life and govern individual behavior in a harsh setting that was often beyond their physical control.

The Secularizing Force of Westernization

As European colonizers began to bring the Arctic under their economic and political control beginning in the 16th century, the governments mobilized missionaries not only to evangelize, but also to "civilize" the inhabitants of their new territories.[325] Christian missionaries were the primary agents of cultural change among the Inuit, but it was not the gospel message that brought the most profound changes to the Inuit worldview of Fear/Power, but rather the secularizing influence of the modern European worldview.

The Christian message itself was not incompatible with the ancient Inuit worldview. As Georges has argued, the themes of fear and power are critical threads in the scriptural gospel story.[326] A clearly-presented gospel message would not cause the Inuit to abandon their beliefs regarding the power of the spiritual world, but would rather affirm their existing worldview by acknowledging the existence of an all-powerful, loving Creator who offers salvation and deliverance to His people from the power of the evil spirits that seek to harm and enslave them (Genesis 3:15, Col. 2:15).

Indeed, the testimony of Fred Savok's grandparents demonstrates that this was the exact effect that the gospel message had when it was first presented to them. He recounts how his grandparents first encountered the gospel through the Evangelical Covenant missionary David Johnson in the late 1800s. Intriguingly, the local shamans had been speaking for some time about a "'very powerful light' coming from the South" that was "much stronger than their own."[327] Shortly prior to the encounter with Johnson, Savok's grandfather Egaq had himself had a dream along these lines:

> He saw a man dressed in white descending and stopping about three feet off the floor in their igloo. "I am the Father of All People," said this person dressed in white. "Soon all people will hear about me." And that was all the unusual person said.[328]

---

[325] Larry Jorgenson, "From Shamans to Missionaries: The Popular Religiosity of the Inupiaq Eskimo," *Word & World*, vol. 10, no. 4, 339-348, 344.
[326] Georges, 42-43.
[327] Savok, 55.
[328] Savok, 56.

As Egaq and his wife Qutleruq puzzled over the meaning of this vision, Johnson and his Inupiaq interpreter, Uyagaq, passed by their cabin on dogsled and stopped to pay them a visit. That night, after a hospitable meal, the visitors shared the gospel message. It is interesting to note that Savok records the message as being presented in clear Guilt/Innocence terminology:

> The Egaqs heard for the first time that there were bad things, called sins, in their hearts. But that God in His love for people sent His Son, Jesus, who can wash bad things away from their lives for better living.[329]

However, as he retells his grandparent's response of faith to the message, it is clear that they understood and processed the message in terms of their own Fear/Power perspective:

> As the days went by, the couple dwelled less on fear, but more on anticipation of a better life. God's stronger power surely must be true, they reasoned... Although the Egaqs had not, as yet, realized it, they had become slaves to the Savior. Slavery to Satan and superstition was left behind.[330]

Savok's grandparents, and to some extent their broader Inupiat culture as a whole, had been supernaturally prepared for the arrival of the gospel message, and as they internalized it and discussed it among their own people, the theme that was consistently emphasized was God's power to deliver them from their fear:

> The Egaqs were often asked to relate their experience and knowledge of the power stronger than that of the Shaman. Constant fear of the Devil and the Shaman were the driving force to embrace the more powerful force of freedom. Naturally, the Shaman opposed the spread of the Good News.[331]

So the gospel message was presented to the Inuit using Guilt/Innocence terminology, but was accepted and culturally processed from within the existing Fear/Power framework.

Contemporary anthropologists have noted and affirmed this continuity between the ancient Inuit worldview and the worldview of the Bible:

> The belief in many devils is not only an aboriginal residue, but is actually in perfect conformity with the version of Christianity now presented to these people. Several missionaries in the region preach of the physical existence of devils. Furthermore, the Eskimo believe that shaman's helping powers were

---

[329] Savok, 58.
[330] Savok, 59-60.
[331] Savok, 74.

real spirits and, by implication, that the shamans actually performed the feats they claim.[332]

Laugrand & Oosten recount what missiologists would call a "power encounter" between a shaman named Angmalik and two Anglican missionaries, which led to a mass-conversion to Christianity in the Cumberland Sound area of present-day Nunavut.[333] They go on to discuss the shamans' conversion to Christianity in terms of fear and power:

> The conversion to Christianity of angakkuit [shamans] implied that they could freely discuss their knowledge and practice without having to fear that they would lose their power by disclosing these things. Their adoption of Christianity, however, did not imply that their belief in angakkuuniq [shamanism] had disappeared. It only implied that they no longer practised it, many shamans having decided to send their tuurngait [helping spirits] away.[334]

Chance argues that some continuity can and should be seen between the shamans' ceremonies of yesterday meant to ensure a good hunt, and the contemporary prayer services in the Christian church that have replaced them.[335] In this sense, the Inuit can still be said to rely on supernatural power for success in the hunt, but the source of that power has shifted from pleasing the spirits to entreating the Creator. Laugrand & Oosten conclude that in Nunavut, "many Inuit considered the missionaries to be shamans," and "may also have seen the Christian religion as a superior form of shamanism."[336] In the evaluation of anthropologist Dorothy Jean Ray, Jesus' power over the spirit world gave Him the status of "super shaman" in the eyes of the Inupiat of the late 1800s.[337]

It was not the arrival of the gospel message itself that brought a cultural shift away from Fear/Power orientation. Rather, it was the secularizing influence of Western culture that caused this shift. To be clear, it was frequently the very same missionaries who brought the gospel in one hand, and a secularized worldview in the other. In Alaska, for example, the federal government viewed the missionary enterprise as an effective means of "civilizing" her new inhabitants, and provided funding to establish schools to educate Inuit children

---

[332] Chance, 59-60.
[333] Laugrand & Oosten, 42-43.
[334] Laugrand & Oosten, 53.
[335] Chance, 40.
[336] Laugrand & Oosten, 65.
[337] Dorothy Jean Ray, *The Eskimos of Bering Strait, 1650-1898* (Seattle: University of Washington, 1975) 251.

and new economic opportunities such as reindeer herding to encourage a transition away from the nomadic subsistence lifestyle.[338]

The missionaries and government agents also brought new diseases. These epidemics wrought havoc on Inuit communities and accelerated the secularization process. Napoleon paints a chilling picture that highlights the powerlessness of the shamans to counter this new-found threat:

> Soon whole families were dead, some leaving only a boy or girl. Babies tried to suckle on the breasts of dead mothers, soon to die themselves. Even the medicine men grew ill and died in despair with their people, and with them died a great part of *Yuuyaraq*, the ancient spirit world of the Eskimo.[339]

As Napoleon tells it, it was this widespread cultural trauma that, more than any other factor, brought about the transition away from the Fear/Power framework. The shamans died or were rendered powerless, and agents of Western culture—whether missionaries or schoolteachers—stepped in to fill the void:

> The survivors also turned over the education and instruction of their children to the missionaries and the school teachers. They taught them very little about *Yuuyaraq*. They allowed the missionaries and the school teachers to inflict physical punishment on their children; for example, washing their children's mouths with soap if they spoke Yup'ik in school or church. Their children were forbidden, on pain of "serving in hell," from dancing or following the old ways.[340]

In terms of social structure within Inuit villages, pastors and schoolteachers effectively replaced the role of the shaman within a few short years.[341]

Along with Western education and its anti-supernatural bias came Western technology. This, too, had an impact on the Fear/Power dynamic. Chance, for example, discusses the impact of the hunting rifle:

> Although the use of the rifle made hunting easier, it... brought into question the validity of the traditional religion by raising doubts about the importance of certain rituals and taboos connected with hunting. This questioning of religion affected the traditional means of social control in that the threat of supernatural punishment for deviation from approved Eskimo practices lost much of its force.[342]

---

[338] Jorgensen, 344.
[339] Napoleon, 11.
[340] Napoleon, 13.
[341] Jorgensen, 345.
[342] Chance, 2-3.

The Danish anthropologist Knud Rasmussen recorded similar reflections from a Canadian Inuk named Ikiliniq in 1931:

> Now that we have firearms it is almost as if we no longer need shamans, or taboo, for now it is not so difficult to procure food as in the old days. Then we had to laboriously hunt the caribou at the sacred crossing places, and there the only thing that helped was strictly observed taboo in combination with magic words and amulets. Now we can shoot caribou everywhere with our guns, and the result is that we have lived ourselves out of the old customs. We forget our magic words, and we scarcely use any amulets now. The young people don't. See, my chest is bare; I haven't got all the bones and grave-goods that the Netsilingmiut hang about them. We forget what we no longer have use for. Even the ancient spirit songs that the great shamans sing together with all the men and women of the village we forget, all the old invocations for bringing Nuliajuk up to earth so that the beasts can be wrested from her – we remember them no more.[343]

Similar effects can be traced through the introduction of medicine, agriculture, transportation, and market-based economics.

So it was not the gospel message itself that prompted the Inuit to transition away from their traditional means of social control. Though it did prompt a reevaluation of their historical taboos, life was still very much understood to take place in a spiritual realm, and the Fear/Power dynamic remained central for the earliest believers. Rather, it was the increasing secularization of the society—brought about through the death of the traditional leaders, the implementation of Western education, and the implicit anti-supernatural bias strengthened by Western technology—that prompted the traditional means of social control to change.

Contemporary Culture: Social Control through Honor & Shame

As the "old ways" passed away and a secularized worldview began to take root, one might assume that the traditional mechanisms of social control would simply be replaced by Western ones. In terms of Muller's three cultural "building blocks," the Fear/Power dynamic would then be replaced by the Western emphasis on Guilt/Innocence. Human behavior would no longer be governed by supernatural spirits or a supreme deity, but rather by an individual sense of "right" and "wrong" and a desire to conform to internal moral codes and external public laws. However, an evaluation of contemporary Inuit culture reveals that this is not the case.

---

[343] Knud Rasmussen, *The Netsilik Eskimos: Social Life and Spiritual Culture*, vol. 8 (1-2) of *Report of the Fifth Thule Expedition 1921-24* (Copenhagen: Gyldendalske Boghandel, 1931). Quoted in Laugrand & Oosten, 11.

The secularization of Inuit culture did not cause a widespread transition to the Western orientation of Guilt/Innocence, but rather "uncovered" and brought into prominence another dynamic of social control that had always existed beneath the surface. Though the earlier analysis of oral history and anthropological studies has identified Fear/Power as the *primary* dynamic of social control in early Inuit culture, it is important to note Muller's word of caution:

> We must be careful, however, not to try and fit each culture or worldview into one specific category… all three building blocks are present in all cultures and worldviews, but how much of each one is present, determines the actual type of culture that emerges.[344]

He goes on to make a specific suggestion about the indigenous cultures of North America, suggesting that they often consist "of elements of both shame-based and fear-based cultures."[345] This is consistent with the observations of Paul Hiebert, who identifies strong elements of both Fear/Power *and* Shame/Honor in what he calls "small-scale oral societies."[346]

Returning to the sources consulted earlier, it is clear that an "undercurrent" of Shame/Honor complimented the dominant value of Fear/Power. This is illustrated again through the story of Qutleruq, who had killed her father by breaking the taboo against making braids. The result of her actions was ostracism from the community: "Qutleruq was now an outcast, labeled a 'murderer.' Yes, labeled as such, even by the whole village. The verdict given by a mother's authority was final. It has been spoken."[347] Qutleruq struggled with this brand of shame throughout her life. It later caused her to be rejected by her mother-in-law as a source of bad luck:

> Like any other mother who loved her children, Egaq's mother could sense the turmoil in her son's life. She, too, after this length of time, learned to love her daughter-in-law. But the fear of breaking rules of superstition was stronger. After the second baby came and died, she encouraged her son to leave his wife who was still in the snow shelter. This would be the quickest way to solve problems coming their way. Surely, the outcast in their family was the source of it all.[348]

---

[344] Muller, 16.
[345] Muller, 20.
[346] Hiebert, *Transforming Worldviews*, 106-111.
[347] Savok, 21.
[348] Savok, 32.

In Qutleruq's story, the dynamics of Fear/Power and Honor/Shame are seen to be working hand-in-hand: honor and shame were observed by the community in order to avoid supernatural consequences.

Anthropologists affirm this communal orientation. Survival for the Inuit depended not only on supernatural power, but also on connectedness to other human beings through a widespread network of kinship for support and mutual sustenance:

> Under this arrangement, all Eskimo who called each other by real or fictive kinship terms assumed a relation of sharing and cooperation (the extent of obligation depending on degree of distance from ego), and were seen by outsiders as being responsible for the actions of the entire kin group. Feuds occasionally arose between these groups and when the conflict resulted in murder, retaliation required the joint action of the appropriate kin members.[349]

Status and face in the community were nearly as important for survival as spiritual power and influence. Sharing, caring, and hospitality were of paramount importance, and thievery and dishonesty were the greatest transgressions; "Any Eskimo found with the bad habit of either one was known by people in several communities. Distrust of such a person among the honest and truthful was, in itself, enough punishment and warning to others."[350] These are clear examples of Shame/Honor values as demonstrated by Georges & Baker.[351]

As the forces of Western secularization removed the dynamic of Fear/Power, this secondary orientation towards Honor/Shame has risen to the surface, and now operates as the primary dynamic of social control in rural Inuit society. Napoleon relies heavily on shame-based language to describe the effects of the cultural transition upon his Yup'ik people. He argues that the death of the "old ways" brought a great sense of communal shame:

> The survivors seem to have agreed, without discussing it, that they would not talk about it. It was too painful and the implications were too great. Discussing it would have let loose emotions they may not have been able to control. It was better not to talk about it, to act as if it had never happened, to *nallunguaq*. To this day *nallunguaq* remains a way of dealing with problems or unpleasant occurrences in Yup'ik life. Young people are advised by elders to *nallunguarluku*, "to pretend it didn't happen."[352]

---

[349] Chance, 49.
[350] Savok, 185.
[351] Georges & Baker, 52-60.
[352] Napoleon, 12.

He goes on, discussing how this dynamic has shaped Inuit behavior today:

> The survivors were stoic and seemed able to live under the most miserable and unbearable of conditions. They are quiet, even deferential. They did not discuss personal problems with others. If they were hurt, they kept it to themselves. If they were angry, they kept it to themselves. They were lauded as being so respectful that they avoided eye-to-eye contact with others. They were passive. Very few exhibited their emotions or discussed them.[353]

Examining social control among the Inuit in more recent times, Chance affirms this orientation towards Shame/Honor: "As long as the Eskimo's economic and social security depends on the assistance and support of others, gossip, ridicule, and ostracism can be quite effective in ensuring conformity to group norms."[354] These are often applied formally in the context of the village council, and in extreme cases banishment from the community is not unusual.[355]

In working with Inuit students over the past six years, my (John's) own ethnographic observations support this conclusion. I have often struggled to involve Inuit students in group conversation, since speaking as an individual in a group setting causes one to "stand out" in a situation where group conformity is the traditional value. Conversely, when participation is *invited* by the larger group, students are much more eager to contribute. In one such case, I asked a student why he chose to address a particularly sensitive racial issue in class publicly. He replied, "My friends asked me to share, and I wanted to honor them." In cases where class work is not completed on time, students will often choose not to attend class, rather than to admit that the work is not complete. Family emergencies are common occurrences due to the extended kinship structure, and students have frequently accrued extended periods of absence due to the cultural obligation to honor and assist one's family. All of these observations are examples of a Shame/Honor worldview in action.

While writing this chapter, I (John) had an intriguing glimpse of this system in action when I attended the Alaska Federation of Natives convention with a student of mine. One reason for our visit was to purchase an authentic Yupik-style drum at the artisan market. Craftsmen from across Alaska were present to sell their handiwork. Walking through the market, I observed two vendors selling these drums. I found my student, who had just committed to purchasing a drum from a third vendor, not having seen the other two. Looking at the drum, I could tell that it was of inferior quality compared to the other two drums I had already seen. As we walked towards the ATM to withdraw money for the drum, I showed the student the other two options. He was very excited

---

[353] Napoleon, 19.
[354] Chance, 65.
[355] Chance, 69.

about the second option that we looked at, but even more exciting to him was the third option. As we spoke with the vendor, we discovered that he was the grandfather of a well-known drummer, Byron Nikolai, who was an acquaintance of my student. He ultimately decided to purchase from this vendor. Later, as we continued walking through the market (with drum in hand), we passed by the booth of the first vendor. The vendor pointed to the drum and asked, "So, you found one somewhere else?" My student told how he had encountered the grandfather of his friend Byron. Explaining why he backed out of the verbal agreement with the first vendor, he said, "I wanted to honor the grandfather of my friend." In a Western context, the vendor might have been quite offended by this decision to back out of their verbal agreement. The Inuit vendor, however, seemed to be quite satisfied with my student's explanation. Purchasing from a friend's grandfather was understood to be much more honorable.

These oral traditions, ethnographic studies, and personal observations all suggest that Western colonialism has wrought a paradigm shift within the Inuit worldview. Through the process of secularization, rural communities that once understood life and controlled society through supernatural power have been forced to give up this guiding principle. Honor and Shame now dominate as the major forces of social control in the Inuit cultures. When Europeans arrived with the gospel message, it was quickly accepted and adapted to the Fear/Power cultural orientation. The Inuit of yesterday found in Jesus the power over evil and fear that their own shamans had long sought and predicted. Sadly, this victory was short lived. As that generation succumbed to epidemic and the "old ways" succumbed to Western secularization, the Shame/Honor framework has now emerged as the primary lens through which contemporary generations understand life.

Summary

Through the ethnographic study of Inuit communities in this chapter, an ethnological portrait of Inuit patterns of education, leadership, and social control has been developed. Across the Arctic, several common values for each of these areas tend to be shared by Inuit communities. Educationally, the Inuit tend to learn best through personal relationship, hands-on experience, oral communication, and close connection to the local environment. Inuit leadership styles tend to be informal, dependent upon age or experience, and qualified by both personal character and accumulated knowledge. Leaders—including educators and ministers—tend to be most effective when using means of social control based on the collectivistic sense of honor and shame. Supernatural power is a secondary theme that ought to be addressed intentionally, while emphasis on personal guilt and innocence is least effective.

Table 4.2: Ethnological Characteristics of Inuit Leadership Development

Cultural Domain / Learning Domain	Education		Leadership		Social Control
Being	Relationship	Orality	Character	Informality	Honor & Shame
Knowing	Environment		Knowledge		Innocence & Guilt
Doing	Experience		Experience		Power & Fear

Chapter 5
Relational Leadership Development

Introduction

With an understanding of circumpolar Inuit cultural values pertaining to education, leadership, and social control in place, the pieces are ready to begin assembling a contextualized model for ministry leadership development. To do this, we will apply the various bodies of educational, sociological, and anthropological theory discussed in chapter 2 to the unique portrait of Inuit culture that emerged in the previous chapter. This will be done in two parts, incorporating the related but distinct epistemological systems of "relational" and "narrative" logic. These two systems, we propose, provide a more appropriate framework for leadership development than the analytical approach that has traditionally dominated the Western academy.

This chapter focuses specifically on relational logic, and the next will incorporate narrative logic. Christian transformative learning theory, relational leadership theory, and honor/shame theory all fall into the realm of "relational logic," and each of these will be applied to the leadership development process among the Inuit. As these principles are contextualized according to the ethnological portrait achieved in chapter 4 and subsequently applied to the leadership development process, a model for relational ministry leadership development among the Inuit takes shape.

Christian Transformative Learning Theory

Considered in light of Christian Transformative Learning Theory, the four educational values identified in the previous chapter offer corrective insight for theological education initiatives throughout the Inuit Arctic. If our ultimate goal as educators and disciplemakers is truly transformation of character, and not just transfer of knowledge, then the value of education through relationship, or "relational disciplemaking," should indeed be second nature to us. By modeling and prioritizing biblical relationships, both horizontally (within the community) and vertically (with the triune God), we can provide a foundation for transformative learning in Inuit students that will outperform any academic criteria or metric. The value of learning through experience, too, is evidenced in this relational paradigm, as we take education out of the classroom and into the context of real-life ministry situations where students can focus not just on "knowing," but also "being" and "doing." Abstract discussions about God and His Word will become transformative to Inuit students only insofar as they are able to apply these principles in day-to-day ministry experiences within the community. Similarly, learning through orality, as opposed to literacy alone, encourages verbal processing and discussion in the context of community in which critical reflection and constructive discourse can thrive. Finally, in learning through the environment, students can be ushered into the vertical dimension of communion with the triune God through the splendor of His handiwork that gives testament to His identity and character. By incorporating these indigenous values into our discipleship efforts, we can facilitate genuine transformative learning that is not only scripturally sound, but also contextually relevant.

Relational Learning

Applied to the field of theological education and leadership development, the value of learning through relationship will dictate that personal relationship, rather than academic achievement, must take precedence in the educational process. Without relationship, Inuit students will have little motivation for success. In Kleinfeld's words, Western teachers will need to "reconcile the western ethic of learning for learning's sake or learning for one's own advancement with village students' motivation to learn for the sake of a personal relationship."[356]

Practically speaking, this means that cultivation of community is paramount to the process of theological education. The traditional residential model for higher education, in which students live in dorms and the faculty live off-site and interact with students primarily during class times, is insufficient. Teachers must live in close proximity to students and intentionally cultivate relationships outside the classroom. Recent trends in higher education are only increasing the distance between faculty and students. The rise of the "commuter campus" and the growing number of part-time students pose direct challenges to the cultivation of student-teacher relationships. The two accredited Bible colleges serving the Arctic must think creatively and institute appropriate policies in response to these trends. Informal residential programs such LEaD Alaska and small group Bible studies such as those organized by Ethnos360 in Greenland provide examples of how this value can be incorporated into the curriculum.

This dynamic also calls into serious question the relevance of traditional distance education in the Inuit context. The norm in online classes, for example, is to use impersonal means of communication such as email and discussion boards. These will not be sufficient to cultivate the type of relationship that Inuit students require. Live video conferences combined with week-long intensive seminars and personal visits from the instructor would be more conducive to effective learning through distance education. Perhaps the

---

[356] Kleinfeld, *Effective Teachers*, 19.

emergence of Zoom and similar videoconferencing systems as legitimate educational tools during the global COVID-19 pandemic will provide a more relational platform for distance education.

Experiential Learning

Seminary and Bible college courses tend to rely heavily on lecture and reading to convey content. Granted, this is unavoidable when the subject matter itself is the written Word of God. How might a Bible teacher incorporate more experiential learning into the curriculum? The solution is not to eliminate verbal and written processing from the curriculum, but rather to supplement these approaches with a heavy dose of experiential learning.[357] To use the terminology of discipleship, "application" must play heavily into the curriculum. In traditional seminary curricula, coursework tends to focus primarily on abstract theological reflection and inductive interpretation of the biblical text. The assumption is often that "application" is done by the student in the field, either during a formal internship or upon graduation.

A curriculum that is contextualized for Inuit discipleship should instead incorporate "field work" as an early and significant component of the education process. Students should spend just as much time working alongside their teachers in actual ministry contexts as they do in the classroom environment. This may lend itself more naturally to a church-based training curriculum where students can be mentored in a hands-on way by an experienced pastor. The early Moravian model may prove insightful, in which students spent the bulk of their time working in actual ministry assignments, and convened periodically for week-long periods of instruction.[358] Similarly, Uyagaq Rock and Stephan Ivanoff, some of the earliest Inuit leaders in the Evangelical Covenant Church, were not trained in the classroom context, but rather learned the ropes of ministry by accompanying the missionaries in their travels and translating for them as they taught the Word of God throughout the region.[359] The INO churches of Greenland employ a similar approach today by mentoring prospective pastors under established missionaries.

In addition to heavy emphasis on application through field work and "on-the-job training," leadership training programs can cater to this experiential value by exploring alternative means of assessment as opposed to the usual written exams and papers. Comprehension can often be gauged just as easily through a creative project that engages the spatial and perceptual domains, such as a painting, a chart, a model, or an audio/visual presentation. Written research papers are not the only ways to demonstrate mastery of a subject,

---

[357] Kleinfeld, *Intellectual Strengths*, 355-35.
[358] Henkelman & Vitt, 212.
[359] Almquist, 49.

though theological education tends to overemphasize this particular means of evaluation—even though most pastors will never write another research paper after graduation from seminary! These alternative means of assessment will be explored in more detail in the next chapter.

Environmental Learning

The importance of the environment to theological education and discipleship may be less evident to educators steeped in the traditional seminary approach. How does one use the environment to teach theology, and how would the local climate pattern influence discipleship? The *Alaska Standards for Culturally Responsive Schools* offer five guidelines for incorporating environmental learning into the curriculum, two of which are particularly relevant to the topic at hand.

First, "Educators who meet this cultural standard... utilize traditional settings such as camps as learning environments for transmitting both cultural and academic knowledge and skills."[360] This guideline can be applied simply by acknowledging that the classroom is not always the ideal environment for theological education. Jesus Himself was a master of using the surrounding environment as a teaching tool. His most famous sermon took place on a mountainside (Matthew 5:1), and some of His greatest lessons were delivered in fishing boats (Matthew 8:23-27, 14:22-33). Contemporary Bible camps emphasize the value of studying God's Word in the context of the natural world. This cultural value can easily be acknowledged by intentionally moving some elements of instruction out of the classroom and into the campgrounds, fishing boats, and hunting cabins that have long provided a natural cultural context for transmission of knowledge.

The second guideline states, "Educators who meet this cultural standard... provide integrated learning activities organized around themes of local significance and across subject areas."[361] The Bible has a great deal to say on the themes of creation and the environment—this line of teaching has simply not been adopted as a major theme in our Western systematic theologies. Christopher Wright, for example, has recently offered a helpful reminder of this neglected theme.[362] The Inuit cultures may be well-positioned to offer prophetic critique of Western theology in this regard. Study of scriptural teaching on the land, the environment, and creation care is one way of incorporating this value into contemporary curricula and encouraging indigenous theological development in areas that are particularly relevant to the local context.

---

[360] *Alaska Standards*, 10.
[361] *Alaska Standards*, 10.
[362] Christopher Wright, *The Mission of God* (Grand Rapids: InterVarsity, 2006). 397-420.

Relational Leadership Theory

Relational Leadership Theory (RLT) emphasizes that leadership can flow in any direction and need not be defined according to official roles. This makes it uniquely suited to contexts of informal leadership such as exemplified by Inuit society. Moreover, since it is not concerned with individual *roles—umialik*, elder, or even pastor—but rather with the *process* of leadership as it is played out through the relational network, RLT is appropriate in the collectivistic orientation of Inuit culture. Uhl-Bien's understanding of leadership as a "social influence process" is consistent with the portrait of leadership that emerged through study of Inuit leadership patterns, in which "The person's character and abilities as valued by the culture determined the degree of *influence over the group.*"[363]

Here the RLT framework is applied specifically to the Inuit community by identifying the various relationships that contribute to the leadership development process. In other words, "What are the relational (social) processes by which leadership emerges and operates?"[364] The ethnographic data surveyed in chapter 4 are organized according to various relational categories to answer this question.

Relationships with Family

In traditional Inuit society, leadership was localized in the kinship unit. The older generation were the leaders of today, and the younger generation were the leaders of tomorrow. Each person was responsible to contribute to the survival of the family unit. A person gradually gained a reputation as a leader through this experience. One who proved industrious, hardworking, and successful at hunting could attain the status of *umialik* or *nukalpiak*, and in later years hold much sway over family affairs as an elder.

Relationships with Community

Though kinship networks continue to be important, contemporary Inuit society extends more broadly to the local community, often known as the "village," than it did in the past. Many of the same dynamics that determine leadership potential within the family apply to the community on a broader level—a person earns influence by developing awareness of and responding to needs within the community. Involvement in and assistance with community events, such as dance festivals and potlucks, provide further such opportunities.

---

[363] Ridley 64, emphasis mine.
[364] Uhl-Bien, 666.

Relationships with Elders

Relationships with elders continue to be of paramount importance in Inuit society. A person who dishonors or disregards elders is marginalized, having very little influence in the family or community. A good leader must be willing to listen to the elders, and this must be demonstrated before a leadership role is recognized. Elders, too, have a responsibility to speak into the lives of the younger generation. Their knowledge and experience, accumulated over the course of many years, provides a foundation for the leaders of tomorrow.

Relationships with Mentors and Instructors

Knowledge is an important leadership value among the Inuit. To know, one must generally be taught. Traditionally, most learning took place in the home through one's parents. Peers and siblings could also serve as teachers during certain activities. Specialized skills might also be taught by an expert who had mastered the craft. In order to become a successful hunter or whaler, for example, a person must be willing to listen to and learn from instruction. As Langdon noted earlier, those in a position to receive more training were in better position to attain the role of *umialik*. The informal term "mentor" might capture best the nature of traditional instruction. Today, the local schoolteacher is an important figure in most villages, and a person's reputation in school may be an indicator of leadership potential. Informal mentors and formal instructors both play important roles in contemporary leadership development.

Relationships with Spiritual Leaders

In ancient times, the shaman played an important role in mediating a person's relationship to the supernatural realm. The shaman contributed to social order by providing a sense of security in an uncertain and harsh environment. His rituals to ward off evil spirits and to entreat good ones brought confidence to daily activities. Conversely, the individual could either contribute to or detract from this sense of social order by observing or ignoring the taboos and rituals. Both parties in the relationship contributed to leadership (as defined by emerging social order) in the community. The shaman also had opportunity, perhaps more than any other party, to provoke cultural change through his spiritual insight.

It has been argued that today, the missionary and/or pastor has filled this same niche. The message of Christ has brought deliverance from fear and superstition and provides hope and confidence for the community through times of uncertainty. Still, the individual participates in this leadership process according to their receptivity and participation in the missionary's message.

Relationships with the Congregation

The establishment of churches in Inuit communities leads to a new relational axis that has important bearing on the question of church leadership—relationships within the congregation, or the local community of believers. This relationship goes beyond the relationship to the broader village by providing opportunities for the exercise of spiritual gifts. The congregation is responsible to recognize and affirm these gifts by allowing individuals to use and develop them. Experience—including trial and error—was traditionally an important aspect of Inuit learning. Hunting, fishing, sewing, leatherworking—all were learned through guided experience and practice. Again, leadership goes both ways—the congregation develops the individual believer, and the believer builds up the body of Christ as the spiritual gifts are exercised with increasing effectiveness. The congregation provides an ideal atmosphere for leadership to be developed and recognized informally as believers "grow into" their leadership potential by proving themselves through experience and character.

Relationships with the Environment

As observed by Paul Hiebert, the mechanistic root metaphor that dominates the dualistic, analytical worldview of Western modernity generally precludes social scientists from considering nonhuman entities through the lens of interpersonal relationships.[365] Hiebert contrasts this with the medieval European worldview, in which people "saw the world as full of living beings interacting with one another. God created it, and it included angels, humans, animals, and other beings, all relating to one another."[366] Similarly, the Inuit traditionally viewed the surrounding environment from a relational perspective. "Survival depended on correct relationships with animals, which were considered as sentient and conscious beings."[367] Egede, for example, summarizes this dynamic in Greenland:

> The factors which determined when one went to work were these: the season, which determined the temperature, the light and the type of game that could be hunted; the tide, which determined where one could meet the animals—and finally the weather, which at any time either made it possible or impossible to go hunting. This was then an organic participation in the nature and the climate, which made the western divisions of time meaningless.[368]

---

[365] Hiebert, *Transforming Worldviews*, 156.
[366] Hiebert, *Transforming Worldviews*, 155.
[367] Laugrand & Oosten, xix.
[368] Egede, 5-6. Emphasis mine.

The dual influences of Christianization and secularization have eliminated most of the traditional *pitaliniit* (taboos) that were meant to appease the *tarniit* (souls) of the animals. Nevertheless, Laugrand & Oosten emphasize that the Inuit continue to prioritize respect for animals and the land:

> The notion of tarniq was integrated into Christianity in the concept of soul. The missionaries assumed that only human beings had a soul and that animals did not have one. Inuit accepted this view, but they continued to respect animals and the land. Today, the ritual rules have been replaced by the moral obligation to respect animals. But the relations human beings have with the land and prey are still perceived as the foundation of Inuit culture and society.[369]

It is notable that the *Inuuqatigiit* curriculum developed for public K-12 education in Nunavut devotes an entire section to "Relationship to the Environment."[370] The local environment contributes to leadership development by honing a leader's skills and character to operate within the physical and spiritual context set by the Creator. An effective Inuit leader is not one who masters or controls the environment, but who understands it, respects it, and uses it appropriately for the good of the community.

Relationship with God

The final two relational categories focus on human relationships with the supernatural. These two are discussed last in this section because they are not considered in most contemporary leadership models. However, a person's relationship to the supernatural realm was of utmost importance to the ancient Inuit and remains so in Christian communities today. It may go without saying that a person's relationship to God has important bearing on leadership development within the church. A person's character is of utmost importance to the question of leadership within Inuit society, and a person whose character does not reflect the community's ideals has little influence. In the church, the character of God is the measure of personal character, and only by nurturing a relationship with God can one's character be conformed to His. To reflect the importance of this "vertical" relationship in the Christian discipleship process, it must be elevated to the top of the list in the model that develops.

Relationships with Demons

The Inuit have always been aware of and attuned to the influence of evil spirits in day-to-day life. Shamans were revered as spiritual leaders because of their ability to ward off evil and communicate taboos that would keep it at bay.

---

[369] Laugrand & Oosten, 132. Emphasis mine.
[370] NT Department of Education, Culture, and Employment, 88-151.

Though the message of the gospel has brought deliverance from much of this day-to-day fear, demonic influence remains a real factor in Inuit life. Today this is often manifested through cycles of depression, alcoholism, and violence. These are often the primary factors that hinder believers from being recognized as leaders... and for those who do begin on the path to ministry leadership, these often lead to their demise. Though social factors also play into these issues, spiritual warfare and victory over evil spirits is an important element of healing and recovery.

Honor-Shame Theory

The importance of honor and shame as tools of social control in Inuit culture are at odds with the Western approach to higher education, which developed out of and is still generally conducted from within a Guilt/Innocence framework. The system is built around the concept of individual performance and achievement, rewarding good academic behavior and punishing poor. R. Quinn Duffy's critique of public education in Nunavut, Canada, is equally relevant to the traditional seminary approach to ministry leadership training:

> For too long and in too many classes Inuit were made to study materials and respond to motivations based on the alien culture of white, middle-class North America. The school system attempted to introduce them to a value system that stressed individual achievement, advancement, and self-discipline in return for future rewards. This orientation often contradicted native values.[371]

Ann Vick-Westgate demonstrates this tension between Honor/Shame and Innocence/Guilt frameworks at work within the Kativik School Board of the Nunavik region in northern Quebec:

> In the Anngutivik newsletter article (Fall/Winter 1988-89) reporting on the Secondary Conference, a teacher representing the Sautijuit School in Kangirsuk discussed that staff's concern that the KSB secondary programs were "geared to the same goal for all students—to achieve academically. Students who graduate are held up as role models to follow. Students who don't graduate, who have 'failed,' are made to feel left out and inadequate. Among Inuit there was never a feast that was meant just for good hunters and their families."[372]

---

[371] R. Quinn Duffy, "Providing an Education," *The Road to Nunavut: The Progress of the Eastern Arctic Inuit since the Second World War* (Montreal: McGill-Queen's University, 1988), 177-78. Quoted in McGregor, 76.
[372] Vick-Westgate, 124.

All of this raises the question, "What does ministry leadership development look like when approached from an Honor/Shame perspective?"

This question, of course, does not have a universal answer, because each culture will have its own expectations regarding honorable and shameful behavior. James Plueddemann provides an example of this from his teaching in East Asian cultures, which often expect a high degree of power distance between teachers and students.[373] In these contexts, classroom decorum is of high importance, and displays of vulnerability on the part of the teacher would be considered embarrassing and dishonorable. However, as Kleinfield's study demonstrated above, the "flat," nearly egalitarian structure of Inuit social hierarchy demands a low power distance in the classroom (as well as in the church). In this context, teachers are expected to cultivate strong interpersonal relationships with students outside the classroom, which provide a relational foundation that motivates students to honor their teachers through good academic performance. Robert Ferris contrasts this against the traditional protocol of the seminary environment, where

> Students typically have little contact with teachers outside the classroom. If the exigencies of life intrude on instruction, this is cause for apology, at least, and potentially for dismissal. A teacher's life may be in crisis, but his problems should not distract students from their intellectual tasks.[374]

This approach is clearly at odds with Inuit cultural values, and Ferris goes on to demonstrate that it is equally at odds with a biblical approach to discipleship:

> Jesus' approach to developing disciples was intensely relational. His commission to the church was to make disciples, not to train scholars. Knowledge is important—God has given us the Scriptures because there is much we need to know—but wisdom and spiritual maturity are nurtured in sustained and open relationship.[375]

The principles of honor and shame provide another strong reminder that relationships must be central to leadership development among the Inuit.

The collectivistic orientation of Inuit society has important bearing on honor in the classroom. As noted above, Western classrooms tend to emphasize the individual over the group. Since Inuit society prioritizes group collaboration for mutual survival, students often prefer to be seen as part of the community

---

[373] James E. Plueddemann, *Leading Across Cultures: Effective Ministry and Mission in the Global Church* (Downers Grove: InterVarsity, 2009). 62
[374] Robert Ferris, "Leadership Development in Missions Settings," in *Missiology: An Introduction to the Foundations, History, and Strategies of World Missions* (Nashville: B&H, 2015), 457-470. 460.
[375] Ferris, 461.

rather than standing out on their own. From a pedagogical perspective, this means that putting individual students in the "spotlight"—to answer questions, think on the spot, or to highlight individual achievement—can be seen as dishonorable. Instead, instructors can teach to the collectivistic identity by emphasizing group work and addressing the class as a whole. Plueddemann notes that "In collectivistic cultures, praising the group is more appropriate than honoring an individual."[376] In traditional academic settings, this might require instructors to break the classroom up into smaller groups, as Douglas Hanson found effective when working with collectivistic Melanesian seminary students.[377] In most of the contexts relevant to this particular study, group sizes will already be small enough, and the teacher's greater challenge might be to gather enough students to avoid a one-on-one teaching situation in which the individual student might feel singled out. We might recall here, for example, Anne-Marit Skare's emphasis on teaching chronologically through the Bible in small groups. Mikeska argues,

> One-to-ones are great ways to make-disciples, however, I am concerned that if we only set our focus on one-to-one then we will miss some of the opportunities that open up with the ability for non-Christians or less mature Christians to join into our lives and relationships which is what LLDM is all about. LLDM focuses on allowing non-Christians, new Christians, mature Christians, or anyone else to be a part of a life on life relationship with Christians.[378]

One strategy that LEaD Alaska has employed when sufficient students could not be recruited is to invite other ministry partners to participate in training sessions to create more of a group dynamic.

The principles of honor and shame also have implications for interpersonal communication between those involved in the leadership development process. Negative behavior cannot be ignored—whether it is poor academic performance in the classroom, or patterns of sin in a disciple's personal life. In the previous chapter, I (John) recounted an instance in which I attempted to exhort a student to take his academic work more seriously. "You need to decide whether you really want to be here," I said, using a blunt confrontational approach that I had found effective with Caucasian students. This Yup'ik student, however, simply excused himself from my office without a word. I had heaped an enormous load of shame on him by calling out his behavior so openly and aggressively. An indirect approach would have been far more effective

---

[376] Plueddemann, 64.
[377] Douglas Hanson, "Preparing Melanesians for Missions," in *Transforming Teaching for Mission: Educational Theory and Practice* (Wilmore: First Fruits, 2014), 247-263. 253.
[378] Mikeska, 113.

here. I could have told a story, or provided an example from my own life or an analogy from the natural world, that would have driven the same point home. In a different instance with another Inuit student, I discovered a blatant case of plagiarism in one of their class assignments. On this occasion, I took a more indirect approach, simply asking the student to meet with me about the paper. As we sat down, I could tell the student was very nervous, and I simply asked, "Do you know why I needed to talk to you?" After that, all I needed to do was listen as the student admitted what they had done and asked for my forgiveness.

This example of plagiarism leads to a final area in which the principles of honor and shame can inform the leadership development process, and this is the domain of mental, emotional, and spiritual health. It is crucial that any ministry leadership development program include specific components to help students address the blanket of shame that so easily smothers potential leaders in Inuit communities. Anne-Marit Skare, for example, alluded to this need in Greenland when she recounted that some of her students "needed counseling before they could take in the biblical message… because of their difficult childhoods."[379] Her own graduate degree in counseling was a tremendous resource in this regard. Anthropologists and Inuit leaders alike have called attention to how the rapid cultural transition and communal trauma has led to a cycle of shame and violence in many Inuit communities.

> The Eskimo youth is expected to be self-reliant in a physical and supernatural world over which he has little control. He must be friendly even with those people he may dislike. He should maintain a sense of pride but remain modest, be prepared for action but have patience. We may assume that these long-continued frustrations build up impulses toward aggression in the individual. Since others strongly condemn any overt expression of these feelings, the individual simply suppresses them (that is, they seldom come to his conscious awareness) except during sudden seemingly unexplainable outbursts of temper during which a mother shouts at her children, or a man beats his wife or destroys someone's property. On rare occasions today, but more frequently in the past, these severe outbursts resulted in murder—or when turned inward, suicide.[380]

These "outbursts" have only increased since Chance wrote in 1966, as Napoleon demonstrates:

> Tragically, under the influence of alcohol and drugs, the pent-up anger, guilt, shame, sorrow, frustration, and hopelessness often is vented through

---

[379] Skare, "Inuit Ministry in Greenland."
[380] Chance, 78.

outbursts of violence to self and others. Such acts, which are difficult for others and even for the sufferer to understand, drive him further into the deadly vortex of guilt and shame.[381]

Promoting open, honest communication about the hurts of the past can allow Jesus Christ to heal the shame of the present. Discussing the legacy of shame left by the Great Death in Alaska, Napoleon emphasizes,

> Only communication, honest communication from the heart, will break this down, because inability to share one's heart and feelings is the most deadly legacy of the Great Death. It was born out of the survivors' inability to face and speak about what they had seen and lived through. The memory was too painful, the reality too hard, the results too hard to hear. Without knowing it, the survivors began to deal with the difficulties of life by trying to ignore them, by denying them, by not talking about them. This is the way they raised their children and their children raised us the same way. Holding things in has become a trait among our families and our people. The results have been tragic.[382]

A Western approach might encourage students to seek individual counseling to address these mental health issues, perhaps even retaining the services of a licensed counselor to see individual students, as Alaska Christian College does through New Hope Counseling Center.[383] Group therapy, however, may provide a more culturally-relevant approach. Napoleon proposes the creation of "Talking Circles" in each village to promote open, honest communication that will allow healing to take place.[384] A church or leadership training program could easily incorporate such a group program to provide a forum for relational healing that can model how to address shame. To be sure, such a therapy program may be outside the training and skillset of many pastors and missionaries, and its details are beyond the scope of this book. Therefore, partnership with counselors and ministries that are familiar with the Inuit culture and qualified to provide such services is an important aspect of the contextualized Inuit leadership development program.

Towards a Relational Model

Having evaluated the traditional approach to theological education in light of key cultural values that play into the Inuit leadership development process, the shortcomings of the traditional approach become more evident. The Bible

---

[381] Napoleon, 15.
[382] Napoleon, 27.
[383] *ACC Academic Catalog*, 12.
[384] Napoleon, 27.

college model removes a person from the community and from the relational network in which learning occurs most naturally, leadership is traditionally recognized, and social influence is earned. The family, the community, the pastor, and the congregation all lose their opportunity to speak into and acknowledge the disciple's development as a leader. The disciple is placed into an artificial community where it becomes more difficult to earn the necessary experience. The leadership development process is essentially boiled down to two relationships—with the instructor and with God. *If*—after having been removed from these key relationships for an extended period of time—a person does return to their community as a candidate for leadership, they return with a good deal of knowledge and a close relationship with God, but very little relevant experience, and—more importantly—the community has been robbed of the opportunity to observe and contribute to the leadership development process. In the words of Bob Lee, the first president of Alaska Bible College, "Potential Native leaders go away to be trained at a formal institution. They return, only to come back and find that a wall has now been erected between them and their own people, thus rendering their leadership largely ineffective."[385]

Gary Ridley closed his dissertation with a recommendation to better engage local churches in the leadership training process:

> Alaska Bible College must develop close ties with the Native churches of Alaska to assure that our educational programs are accessible to potential leaders… Maintaining the servant role, Alaska Bible College ought to stimulate and assist the Native churches to develop local programs for leadership development.[386]

This particular recommendation was never implemented at Alaska Bible College. What follows is an attempt to integrate *all* of the relationships identified above through RLT into a such a localized model for leadership development in the Inuit church.

The relational outline that follows is written from the perspective of the "disciple"—an appropriate theological term for an individual that is undergoing the process of leadership development in the church. This term is used here because the ultimate focus of the current study is to see mature leadership for the Inuit church. Moreover, it is appropriate since most disciples would not necessarily consider themselves to be future leadership candidates—particularly early in the process. All disciples begin their journey as followers, not leaders. Nevertheless, a mature disciple is, according to the definitions and

---

[385] Rempel, 9.
[386] Ridley, 110-111.

assumptions established in chapter 1, a leader. This term, then, nicely captures the multidirectional nature of leadership that characterizes RLT.

Disciple-God

In the discussion of RLT above, the relationship with God was discussed last because of contemporary society's tendency to ignore or downplay the supernatural or "vertical" dimension of relationship. In applying RLT from a distinctly Christian perspective in the emerging model, it is important to move this relationship to the top of the list. As established at length in chapters 1 and 2, it is in the Triune God that all other relationships find their existence and significance. Christian transformative learning begins with "being," and it is "in him [that] we live and move and have our being" (Acts 17:28).

A contextualized leadership development program, then, must focus just as much on character as it does on knowledge and experience. Someone might have all the right information, but without the character to back it up, they will not be accepted as a leader. Christian character develops through a close relationship with God. Thus, a leadership development program must incorporate regular study of God's Word and communication with Him through prayer. Depending on the context and situation, this may happen communally or individually as deemed appropriate. Ideally, this practice would be modeled for the disciple by parents, elders, and the missionary or pastor. In practice, it will likely be the missionary or pastor that is responsible to hold the disciple accountable through a mentoring relationship. This mentoring role will be elaborated in greater detail below, but the focus here is on the gradual transformation of a disciple's character as they are conformed to the image of God.

Disciple-Family

Recognizing the traditional importance of the kinship unit to the leadership process, leadership development for the church today ought also to begin in the family. The Christian family provides the earliest "proving ground" for tomorrow's church leaders. It is incumbent upon Christian parents to model and instill the character qualities that will qualify their children as tomorrow's leaders. Any leadership development program must note that fulfillment of family obligations—which in Inuit society includes the expanded kinship network—has an important bearing on future leadership roles. Common contemporary examples include presence at funerals (including an extended mourning period), visiting family members in the hospital, assisting family members who are "down on their luck" or in transition, and simply being present—especially for younger siblings. As a teacher in a Bible college, inability to fulfill these obligations due to distance and travel expenses was one of the most frequent struggles expressed by my (John's) Inuit students. Indeed,

Paul himself pointed to a person's family affairs as a fundamental criterion for leadership in the church (1 Timothy 3:4-5).

Disciple-Community

A contextualized Inuit leadership development program will engage individuals in their local community. Community involvement not only provides the practical experience that is essential to eventual leadership roles, but also develops important relational "capital" the eyes of community members. Not just any community involvement will do—for example, Alaska Bible College requires all residential students to be involved in community service throughout the course of study. However, since this service takes place exclusively in the local community around the Bible college, the students gain no reputation or influence in their home communities. It is no wonder that so many students who do enroll in Bible college programs never return home. Since it is the community that must ultimately "grant" influence to the individual, it is important that the disciple has regular and intentional contact with that particular community.

One important aspect of community relations is that of vocation. Many rural churches cannot support a full-time pastor, so it is important that potential leaders develop some way to support themselves and their future ministries. This will vary based on the economy of each local village. Vocational training (through partnership with regional vocational programs) may be an important aspect of church leadership development in some contexts, while leaders in other areas may be able to supplement their income through traditional subsistence activities.

Disciple-Elder

Considering the enduring importance of community elders in Inuit social structure, any leadership development program ought to engage elders consistently in the process. This can include village and family elders who help shape pastoral leadership by relaying important local values, traditions, and knowledge, as well as seasoned Christian elders from other ministry contexts who have proven themselves faithful and are known to the community. These relationships can easily be fostered through simple visitation ministry organized and modeled by the pastor or missionary, and through invitations that can be extended to mature Christian elders elsewhere in the region. Through extended local visits, these mature believers have an opportunity to invest in the disciple through simple LLDM as envisioned by Mikeska.

Disciple-Mentor

It should go without saying that missionaries of today ought to be intentionally cultivating relationships with tomorrow's leaders, "working themselves out of a job," so to speak. In the same way, pastors have a responsibility to be actively preparing a new generation of leaders for the church. Sadly, since leadership development in the church is so often equated with formal theological education, most pastors and missionaries feel ill-equipped for this task. This need not be the case.

The bulk of the day-to-day responsibility in developing tomorrow's Inuit church leaders rightfully rests on those same leaders today. This aligns with traditional leadership patterns, in which younger hunters or whalers, for example, gained experience working alongside and learning from the seasoned leaders. A pastor may not feel qualified to train a person in the intricacies of exegesis or homiletics, but these matters of "content" can easily be left to specialized instructors. Instead, the pastor or missionary can focus on engaging disciples in day-to-day ministry activities and basic study of the Scriptures. Taking a younger disciple along when visiting the sick or participating in denominational conferences, for example, will provide valuable ministry experience that can translate into a leadership role in the future. A consistent pattern of mentoring meetings between the disciple and the local mentor forms the backbone of the relational model. These meetings ought to emphasize in equal parts study (oral study of the Scriptures) and practice (ministry activities such as teaching, pastoral care, and visitation).

Disciple-Instructor

Knowledge is an important aspect of leadership in Inuit culture, so instructors will always have an important role to play in the leadership development process. No one could become a good hunter or whaler without training from others. A shaman's role was contingent upon intimate knowledge of the spiritual realm and the accompanying rituals, and in the same way a pastor must be intimately familiar with the Word of God. This is where the traditional model of theological education excels, and is perhaps the most difficult aspect to implement in a more relational context. How can individuals receive the necessary training in the Word of God without being removed from the local community?

Online education is an enticing idea, but its highly independent, non-relational nature is poorly-suited to Inuit learning styles. Historically, the modular format has proven quite successful in Inuit contexts. Periodic, weeklong periods of face-to-face instruction in a central hub seem to offer a good balance between the need for relational learning and the need to remain active and engaged in the local community. Disciples are able to leave their communities for a week at a time for focused learning without sacrificing relationships over the long term. These can be sponsored by a Bible college, a group of churches, or a denomination. In the early- to mid-twentieth century, the Moravian church had good success offering seasonal "Helper Conferences" in this format.[387] The Evangelical Covenant Church's Western Alaska Ministry Training is a good contemporary example.[388]

Thus, it should be emphasized here that there remains an important role for traditional theological education in the development of indigenous leaders. However, these courses must be adapted to meet the needs of localized leadership development patterns. An important question to consider is which topics should be required for pastoral leadership roles in the church. This is a question best answered at the local level, with input from denominational/mission leadership and regional institutions of formal theological training such as Alaska Bible College. The following chapter on orality will further address the pedagogical methods and curricular considerations of these modules.

Disciple-Congregation

If a person is to eventually become a leader in the church, then experience in the church is essential. The most successful leadership development programs in the storied past of Inuit missions were those that engaged individuals in lay leadership roles very early in the process. More recently, as emphasis has shifted to professional pastors and formal training, ministry leaders have become more hesitant to delegate such responsibilities. Coaching individuals through the process of teaching a lesson, leading worship, or hosting a prayer meeting, and being willing to hold such responsibilities "loosely" so that others can gain experience is important to the leadership development process. As Plueddemann observes,

> Most studies show that perspective transformation is not learned through courses on theories of leadership or elaborate management techniques. Perspective transformation develops by reflecting on disequilibrating experiences and through disorienting dilemmas. In other words, leaders don't develop if they don't face challenging situations.[389]

The local congregation provides an ideal context in which to stretch disciples with tasks that are slightly beyond their comfort zone, and then to support them as they carry them out and reflect on the results. In settings such as northern Canada and Greenland, where indigenous Evangelical congregations have yet to take firm root, this dynamic will be more difficult to address.

---

[387] Henkelman & Vitt, 215.
[388] "Western Alaska Ministry Training," *Alaska Conference of the Evangelical Covenant Church*, www.alaskacovenant.org/western-alaska-ministry-training/ (Accessed 25 January 2019).
[389] Plueddemann, 203.

However, even a very small group of believers can be encouraged to gather for prayer under its own indigenous leadership.

Disciple-Environment

The Inuit concept of relationship with the local environment cannot be overlooked in the leadership development process. In Inuit contexts, ministry leadership must be integrated into the local environment. A disciple must be able to discern true scriptural teaching regarding human origins and relationships with the animal world. Effective leaders will also be characterized by respect for the environment and good stewardship of local resources. Mentoring meetings need not always take place in the pastor's study or the missionary's home. As Jesus Himself demonstrates, natural settings such as fishing boats and hunting cabins provide prime settings for discipleship.

Disciple-Demonic

The demonic relationship is the only one to be resisted rather than nurtured (James 4:7). While it is true that the Power/Fear dynamic has been deemphasized in Inuit society over the past century, it remains a powerful undercurrent in the Inuit worldview. From a biblical perspective, a pastor will understand that the forces of evil have not disappeared but simply shifted their tactics from ritual and taboo to shame, depression, addiction, and abuse. Breaking these patterns of demonic oppression is one aspect of leadership development that is likely to be more difficult without relocation. Emotional and spiritual healing may be difficult to achieve without getting away from the "battlefield" for a season. This is one purported strength of the residential Bible college, as students are able to leave behind distractions to focus on God's Word. Even so, simply "getting away" for a while is insufficient in overcoming strongholds of demonic oppression, and it is not unusual for the same struggles to return immediately upon going home.

Spiritual warfare, including recovery from trauma and abuse in the past, should be a part of any Inuit leadership development program. As with Bible training modules, such activities may be most effective when provided off-site in a neutral or spiritually-positive environment. Hearts Going Toward Wellness is an example of one such ministry that provides retreats specifically contextualized for Alaska Native audiences.[390]

On a day-to-day basis, pastors and missionaries must recognize that many disciples are carrying spiritual "baggage" from past trauma and may be susceptible to demonic oppression. They should be ready to support and encourage individuals when it becomes an issue and arrange for counseling resources to support the leadership development program on an ongoing basis.

---

[390] *Hearts Going Toward Wellness*, www.heartsgtwellness.org (Accessed 25 January 2019).

The enemy uses shame with great effect to discourage many Inuit away from leadership roles in the church. Talking circles such as those proposed by Napoleon that address these issues openly and honestly in an environment of love and acceptance can be a helpful tool in the local setting. Ministry leaders must be aware of the potential for relapse and be prepared with an answer for when it occurs. Relapse need not disqualify a person from ministry.

Summary

Traditional Inuit society is characterized by informal leadership in which the community as a whole recognizes and grants influence to those who prove themselves to be good leaders through knowledge, experience, and most importantly, good character. The traditional approach to pastoral training through theological education generally fails to produce indigenous pastors and leaders that fit the needs of Inuit churches. By applying Christian Transformative Learning Theory, Relational Leadership Theory, and Honor-Shame Theory to the question of leadership development, another model emerges that may be more successful in producing Inuit pastors to serve in an informal, relationally-driven context.

The key distinctive of this relational model is that it is centered in the local church, not the residential Bible college or seminary. Though theological education is still important, it is the local pastor or missionary, not the college faculty, that takes the greatest responsibility in overseeing and implementing the leadership development process. This allows leaders to develop and be recognized informally in the local church and community. A degree or certificate is not the focus of this model. Though individual denominations and agencies may wish to issue such certifications for their own record-keeping purposes, these are not important at the local level. Rather, success is demonstrated by the community's informal affirmation and acceptance of an individual's readiness to lead.

The process as envisioned begins in the family, the community, and the local congregation, as character is modeled by the older generation and the younger begin to contribute to society in increasing measure. Children, of course, should not be expected to think of themselves as future leaders, nor should youth be expected to aspire to pastoral roles—this would run counter to the leadership values embedded in the culture. Rather, as they demonstrate leadership potential they are naturally recognized by the community and become candidates for increased responsibility in the church. In what might be considered a local "school of discipleship" (which could easily function with only one or two disciples at a time) the pastor or missionary mentors these individuals towards greater spiritual maturity through the following mechanisms:

1. Regular small group mentoring meetings focusing on oral Bible study, prayer, encouragement, and accountability.
2. Regular, guided ministry responsibilities in the church and community that stretch the individual.
3. Community service activities and vocational training or job skill development (as deemed necessary and in cooperation with other local resources).
4. Visiting with local elders and inviting mature Christian elders from elsewhere.
5. Theological education modules in a regional hub (in partnership with other village churches and regional institutions of theological education).
6. Intentional attention to and use of the local environment as a setting for discipleship, including recreation and participation in subsistence activities.
7. Trauma healing workshops and other group counseling opportunities to promote emotional wellness and to break patterns of demonic oppression.

By design, this model does not provide a complete curriculum or answer all the questions. Rather, it casts a vision for how pastoral training among the Inuit might be accomplished more effectively. It is our prayer that it will provide a starting point for a group of pastors who desire to move their congregations towards indigenous leadership.

Table 5.1: Relational Model for Inuit Leadership Development

Transformative Learning Domain	Relationship between Disciple and...	Cultural Values Addressed	Communal Discipleship Activities
Being	God	Character, Honor & Shame, Power & Fear	Bible study, prayer
	Family	Character, Honor & Shame	Modeling, mentoring
Knowing	Elder	Honor & Shame, Knowledge	Local visitation, hosting mature Christian elders

	Environment	Knowledge, Environment	Excursions, subsistence
	Instructor	Knowledge	Regional training modules
Doing	Congregation	Character, Experience, Informality	Teaching, visitation
	Community	Honor & Shame, Experience, Informality	Community service, subsistence, job skills training
Feeling[391]	Demonic Beings	Power & Fear, Honor & Shame	Talking circles, trauma healing workshops
Integrative[392]	Mentor (Local Pastor or Missionary)	Knowledge, Character, Experience, Informality	LLDM, small-group mentoring, ministry apprenticeship

---

[391] Though "feeling" is not traditionally one of the three domains discussed in transformative learning theory, cultural values should not be constrained to fit theory. Rather, theory ought to be expanded to accommodate cultural realities.

[392] This key relationship is foundational to the leadership development process. Though many of the relationships could be understood to span multiple domains of transformative learning, the local pastor or missionary mentor is uniquely responsible to integrate all aspects of the process from beginning to fruition.

Chapter 6
Orality-based Leadership Development

Introduction

The previous chapter outlined a general structural overview for a relational leadership development program based in a local ministry and overseen by a missionary or pastor. In addition to extensive opportunities for hands-on experiential learning, this program entails a number of components that take place in a more traditional learning environment. These include regular meetings with the mentor for Bible study as well as participation in theological education modules. Trauma healing workshops and vocational training may also have "classroom" aspects. In addition to the relational structure of the overall model described in the previous chapter, it is also important to address the nature and content of these individual components. Attention thus turns to final major educational value that emerged in the ethnology of Inuit leadership development: orality, or "narrative logic."

As we established in chapter 2, relational and narrative logic are intrinsically linked. By nature, relationships generate stories, which in turn provide the Peircean "signs" that allow a relational realist to make a truth claim. Stories in narrative logic are analogous to the propositional statements of analytical logic (which characterizes traditional theological education). Chapter 3 identified several contemporary approaches to discipleship and leadership development that have found success in using narrative-based curriculum among the Inuit. Chapter 4 identified orality as a key Inuit cultural value contributing to the processes of education, leadership, and social control in traditional Inuit culture. In this chapter we will apply narrative logic to the process of Inuit ministry leadership development, exploring how these principles must influence both the pedagogical process and the curricular content.

In her analysis of oral learning, Lynn Thigpen emphasizes that in this context, "orality" denotes not only the source of information (written word vs. spoken word) but also the source of trust (human relationships vs. formal credentials) in the learning process. Using these two variables as axes on a graph, Thigpen plots four different "learning quadrants" to describe learning across cultures.[393] Based on the ethnological profile developed in chapter 4, Inuit learners would tend to fall into the "Primary Orality" quadrant, placing

---

[393] Lynn Thigpen, *Connected Learning: A Grounded Theory Study of how Cambodian Adults with Limited Formal Education Learn* (Ph.D. product, Biola University, 2016). 138.

more trust in human relationships than in formal academic credentials, and having a preference for oral information transfer over the written word. These two axes correspond loosely to pedagogical methods (relational vs. academic) and curricular design (narrative vs. propositional). Both are considered in this chapter, beginning with a consideration of orality-based pedagogical methods, followed by a brief consideration of curricular content.

Orality-based Pedagogy

Whereas the traditional approach to theological education has heavily emphasized literacy, the oral heritage of Inuit learners suggests that reading and writing are not the preferred means of transferring knowledge. Discussions of *Inuit Qaujimajatuqangit* and Native Ways of Knowing all center around a generational transfer of knowledge from a community's ancestors to its youth through the elders. Information is trusted because of relationships, not because of credentials.

The academic classroom, on the other hand, tends to revolve around the textbook. Through the processes of scholarly vetting, peer review, and formal publication, textbooks (and other academic publications) are generally considered the authoritative word on the subject, and students are expected to master them. Instructors put much thought into selecting the right texts for a course, which provide a basis for lecture, discussion, and activities. Instructors will often make a special note on key areas where they "disagree with the textbook."

McIlwain makes an important observation on how this reliance on the printed word can be problematic when attempting to develop leaders in an orality-based culture:

> Many missionaries find themselves dependent on younger men to teach and lead tribal churches because the difference between the young and the old, educated and uneducated, is unnecessarily accentuated by the analytical, topical approach which is taught to them as the primary method of teaching the Word of God. Younger men, however, lack the natural experiences of life which prepare one to be a wise instructor. In many cultures, the young men would not be granted the respect so necessary for a church teacher and leader. Many missionaries can testify to the heartache of seeing young, promising leaders ruined for the ministry through pride, adultery, and a host of other vices and inconsistencies.[394]

If a high degree of literacy and proficiency in analytical thought are requirements for the leadership development process, then the pool of

---

[394] McIlwain, 68.

potential leaders in an oral society becomes artificially shallow. Indeed, the remaining candidates who do meet these criteria may find that they are better suited for leadership in Caucasian churches rather than in their home villages.

Based on current literacy trends in Inuit communities, Church leaders and theological educators must assume that the current generation of adult learners will encounter difficulty with seminary-level textbooks and will prefer to process this information orally. Reading lists will need to be adapted accordingly, with more time given to oral media (including video, where relevant). Whereas Western educators often prefer students to read first and then discuss, it may be more effective for Inuit learners to discuss a topic orally first, and then follow up through guided reading. In many cases, reading can be replaced entirely with oral forms of exegesis.

The format of oral instruction also needs to be considered. Systematic lecture tends to be less meaningful than narrative teaching. Main teaching points can be effectively introduced by telling a story that illustrates the principle being discussed. In traditional learning, stories would often emphasize the importance of the topic at hand.[395] This principle can easily be applied in biblical and theological studies by sharing personal anecdotes that illustrate the relevance of the doctrine or passage being studied to everyday life. Many of the pedagogical methods already suggested in the previous chapter as conducive to relational learning are equally applicable here, including small groups and case studies.

Of course, pedagogy is not a one-way process, and orality also has important implications for how learners will synthesize and retransmit instructional content to demonstrate competency. The typical means of assessment in academic settings are written exams and research papers. These methods are insufficient for oral-preference learners. More appropriate to the Inuit context are oral exams and presentations, which can be administered individually or in group formats.

An oral exam can serve the same purpose as a written exam, but will require some work on the part of the instructor to adapt it for oral administration. Rather than simply reading the questions from the written test aloud to the student and recording their responses, the exam must be rewritten in a conversational format, similar to a written essay test. The instructor should prepare leading questions addressing the core points to be evaluated. Where a student's answer is unclear or insufficient, the instructor can ask follow-up questions that will allow the student to demonstrate sufficient competency. A

---

[395] Angayuqaq Oscar Kawagaley, "Alaska Native Education: History and Adaptation in the New Millenium," in *Alaska Native Education: Views from Within* (Fairbanks: Alaska Native Knowledge Network, 2010). 89.

standardized rubric prepared ahead of time can help the instructor score students' responses consistently.

Oral presentations can take the place of written research papers and may in fact be better suited to preparing students for pulpit-based ministry. Sioux Falls Seminary has recently pioneered the use of the oral presentations as an alternative to the written paper, requiring one minute of presentation time as an equivalent to one written page.[396] This equivalency can allow instructors to give students the option to choose their preferred means of evaluation.

Both exams and presentations can be administered individually or in group contexts. Most instructors will be more familiar and comfortable with the traditional individual approach to grading. However, with some adaptation, instructors can better accommodate the collectivistic orientation of Inuit culture by evaluating students as a group as they work together to complete an exam or assignment. Conversational exams are scalable to include multiple students, just as in everyday conversation. The instructor must take special care to include all students in the conversation. In such a system, a whole class (or specific subgroups of a class) would receive the same grade. This grade would not only reflect the accuracy and quality of the work, but also the level of participation from the whole group.

Evaluation of oral work need not be limited to the instructor. Peer evaluation is a tool with which many homiletics instructors will already be familiar, and may prove helpful in lowering power distance in the classroom and removing some of the social pressure from the instructor-student relationship. Again, Sioux Falls Seminary reports success in using peer evaluation for oral learners.[397]

All of the pedagogical tools mentioned above are basically variations on "tried-and-true" methods already used in academic contexts, but are there any indigenous forms of communication that can be incorporated into the leadership development process? One such example that deserves consideration is the Inuit drum dance. Variations of this traditional art form are still practiced in many communities across the Arctic. The subject matter of these dances generally focuses on daily life. Many describe subsistence activities such as hunting or berry picking, as dancers pantomime the actions of the hunters, the animals, or the berry pickers. More recently composed dances can describe aspects of modern technology.[398] Cynthia Pete, a former student of

---

[396] Larry Caldwell, "Theological Institutions and Orality: Paying Attention to Non-readers at Home and Abroad" (conference presentation at Evangelical Missiological Society Annual Meeting, Dallas, TX, October 9, 2020). https://youtu.be/-5Q1Fytw5bk?t=1455.
[397] Caldwell, https://youtu.be/-5Q1Fytw5bk?t=1368.
[398] Ann Fienup-Riordan, *The Nelson Island Eskimo: Social Structure and Ritual Distribution* (Anchorage: Alaska Pacific University, 1983), 317.

mine (John's) and a Yupik dancer from the village of Stebbins, describes it as "telling stories with your hands."[399] The dances are composed by members the older generation and "given" to a specific younger individual, often to signal a coming-of-age.[400] Popular dances are repeated and incorporated into the community's repertoire, thus contributing to the oral history of the community. In her senior project at Alaska Bible College, Pete argued that the narrative nature of these dances makes them an ideal vehicle for communicating biblical teaching.[401] In 2017, she collaborated with Covenant Youth of Alaska and InterVarsity to host the "Would Jesus Eat Frybread?" conference in Anchorage. At this conference, Mary Huntington, a school administrator and Inupiaq dancer from Shishmaref, demonstrated this by teaching a group of students a dance that she composed titled "My Savior."[402] The lyrics and motions of this song describe the earthly life of Jesus and His impact on the believer. It provides an example that other Inuit students can use to create their own songs and dances that demonstrate the truths learned in the classroom. These in turn can quickly be transmitted to others in their own local communities. Of course, instructors will need to do sufficient background research in their own local communities to determine the extent to which the art form has been preserved and the cultural connotations that it may carry in the local context. However, in the right setting Inuit dancing can provide a culturally relevant means by which students can reflect, synthesize, and retransmit the biblical truths mastered in the classroom.

Narrative-based Curriculum

Going beyond the question of pedagogical methodology, the curricular content of the ministry leadership development process must also be considered. Adjustments to teaching styles and learning activities will only go so far in addressing the needs of oral learners. I (John) am reminded here of a conversation I had early in my tenure as Academic Dean at Alaska Bible College with one of the school's senior administrators. I was arguing the need to incorporate orality into the curriculum in order to better serve Alaska Native students. Though he recognized the need to adapt pedagogical methods where possible, he saw orality as fundamentally incompatible with some of the core components of the college's prescribed curriculum. He asked, "How can I teach PIBS [Principles of Inductive Bible Study] through stories?" This class, which he taught every year using the step-by-step analytical process developed by

---

[399] Cynthia Pete, *A Native Tradition and Christianity* (B.A. product, Alaska Bible College, 2015), 6.
[400] Fienup-Riordan 1983, 317.
[401] Pete, 12.
[402] Mary Huntington, "Saturday PM Session" (conference presentation at Would Jesus Eat Frybread?, Anchorage, AK, November 11 2016). https://youtu.be/HjFlh05omBI?t=1811.

Howard Hendricks, had become his signature course, and he rightly recognized that the class as he approached it would be difficult or impossible to teach using different pedagogical methods. I had no answer for him at the time, but I now understand that we needed to be asking a deeper question—not "How do we teach PIBS using stories," but rather, "How are Bible study methods addressed in a narrative-based curriculum?" As Matthews and Steffen demonstrate, the narrative orientation of the Inuit worldview requires a departure from the systematic and analytical approach to biblical teaching that tends to dominate in the academy.

Granted, the denominational nuances of the ministry leadership development curriculum across a region as large as the North American Arctic are beyond the scope of this study. Each denomination and agency will have different expectations and requirements for its own leadership development curriculum. These might include topics such as denominational polity, church history, original languages, and even competency in certain "general education" topics such as math, science, and language arts. With Steffen's appeal for a "glocal" approach in mind, these nuances are not addressed here, and are left for individual organizations to consider in light of the general principles that we identify.

This discussion on curriculum focuses on the core body of scriptural knowledge and skills in which any ministry leader must possess competency in order to lead a local fellowship of believers. Denominational and cultural differences aside, the foundational guide for any church is the Word of God, which is at the heart of any Evangelical approach to ministry leadership development.

Introduction and Critique of Firm Foundations

There is certainly no need to reinvent the wheel at this point. As surveyed in chapter 3, ministries across the Arctic have already discovered that narrative-based curricular approaches to biblical training are effective among the Inuit. The ethnology in chapter 4 corroborates this experience with ethnographic data from Inuit communities in Alaska, Canada, and Greenland. The most common narrative-based curriculum in use among the Inuit today is the Firm Foundations series developed by Trevor McIlwain of Ethnos360, which is employed by various ministries in all three nations.

Nevertheless, Firm Foundations has its shortcomings. Originally developed by an Australian missionary for ministry among the Palawano people of the southern Philippines, it arose out of a very specific cultural context for a specific purpose.[403] Over the years, McIlwain's notes have been revised and expanded for use by Ethnos360's church planting teams around the globe. According to

---

[403] McIlwain, 9-13.

the foreword, "These volumes are written for any Christian who desires to know and teach the Scriptures."[404] To use Steffen's paradigm, Firm Foundations is a "global" approach, designed to be useful across all cultures and worldviews. It has been translated into many different languages, and a two-credit course titled "Curriculum Development" at Ethnos360's missionary training center emphasizes a thorough study of local culture in order to contextualize the curriculum as needed.[405] One version of the curriculum titled *Firm Foundations: Creation to Christ* is marketed for use as a Bible study in Western churches.[406] It is this version that was used by Anne-Marit Skare in her work in Greenland.[407] Notably, though widely used, Firm Foundations has not been translated into any Inuit language or contextualized for local or glocal use in Inuit communities.

To this end, the remainder of this chapter proposes key revisions to the Firm Foundations curriculum for use in Inuit contexts.[408] As will be demonstrated, some crucial themes in Inuit culture, seen earlier in chapter 4, are not addressed by McIlwain's original 70 Phase 1 lessons. After outlining specific elements that should be added to the lessons to address these themes, the chapter will conclude with some general suggestions on adapting McIlwain's approach to be consistent with the pedagogical findings discussed earlier in this chapter.

To begin this task, it is helpful to start with a broad overview of the curriculum as it currently exists. Tom Steffen has provided a thorough survey of its origins and development over the years, and his summary provides an ideal starting point:

> The first volume, published in 1987, provided the philosophy for the CBT [Chronological Bible Teaching]... The remaining volumes of Firm Foundations were Bible lessons designed specifically for tribal peoples. The evangelism phase (Phase 1) consisted of 68 [70 in the revised edition] Bible stories, 42 from the OT, and 26 from the New Testament (NT). Five other CBT phases followed the evangelism phase. Phase 2 was an abbreviated review of Phase 1, focusing on security of salvation and the young believer's

---

[404] McIlwain, vii.
[405] "Academics – Missionary Training Center (MTC)," *Ethnos360*, https://ethnos360.org/training/missionary-training-center/academics (Accessed 4 November 2020).
[406] Steffen, *Worldview-based Storying*, 84.
[407] Skare, "Inuit Ministry in Greenland."
[408] This discussion is based on the 2005 edition of the curriculum, *Building on Firm Foundations (Revised Edition)*. Compared to the similarly-titled *Firm Foundations: Creation to Christ* mentioned above, *Building on Firm Foundations* is marketed as the cross-cultural edition of the curriculum, containing additional lessons that address themes of Fear & Power often encountered in animistic settings.

newfound position in Christ. They rejoiced that they were no longer separated from the holy God. Phase 3 covered Acts, recounting the history of the early church and setting the foundation for the Epistles. Phase 4 surveyed the Epistles, culminating with Revelation. In a rather short period of time, the listeners were exposed to the metanarrative of Scripture from Genesis to Revelation. Phases 5-7 repeated the cycle focusing on issues of sanctification for the maturing believers.[409]

The proposals that follow in this chapter are based on Phase 1 of the curriculum, which provide the foundation for the entire series. Phase 1 is written with an evangelistic purpose, tracing the thread of God's redemptive story through creation, fall, and restoration. It might be assumed that those participating in a ministry leadership development program are already believers. Nevertheless, the broad narrative arc of Scripture that Phase 1 establishes is a fitting starting point for the curriculum for several reasons: (1) it lays the necessary foundation for further study, (2) it provides an evangelistic model that students can use to communicate the gospel to others, and (3) it encourages students to integrate their understanding of the Christian faith with the Inuit worldview. By focusing on Phase 1 in this proposal, we do not imply that this phase alone is sufficient to develop ministry leaders. Rather, it provides a common "building block" that can be complemented by working through the subsequent phases or through other opportunities for study, as deemed appropriate and helpful by the missionary, pastor, or denominational leadership.

Being written by an Australian working from a distinctive "Innocence/Guilt" cultural framework to a Philippine tribe characterized by a "Power/Fear" orientation, it is no surprise that both of these perspectives feature heavily in the Firm Foundations curriculum. McIlwain summarizes the major themes of Phase 1 as follows:

> The doctrinal themes which are emphasized through Phase 1 are those which will show people they are sinful, condemned, and helpless before God, their holy and righteous Creator and Judge, as well as those which will generate repentance and faith and bring complete dependence on the Lord Jesus Christ as the all-sufficient Savior.[410]

These are clear "Guilt/Innocence" terms with which Westerners are most comfortable using to discuss the Gospel message. McIlwain is also careful to consistently emphasize God's supreme and sovereign character in comparison to the spirit world, which is a part of His Creation:

---

[409] Steffen, *Worldview-based Storying*, 35-36.
[410] McIlwain, 159.

This type of supreme being is foreign to the mind of the animistic tribal person who spends his entire life trying to deceive, manipulate, bribe, or appease the spirits in an effort to keep in an agreeable relationship with them. The animist lives in constant fear of spiritual powers that do not have any right to control him.[411]

Surveying the passages that McIlwain has selected to develop these themes, his emphasis is clear. Twenty lessons cover Genesis 1-11, with seven more to cover the patriarchal period in the remainder of Genesis. Thirteen lessons cover the period of Exodus & Wandering (Exodus-Deuteronomy), in which the themes of law, guilt, sacrifice, and grace are elaborated. Notably, two entire lessons are devoted to the Ten Commandments (Exodus 20:1-17), which is the only biblical narrative to be divided into multiple lessons in the entire volume. Five more lessons cover the remainder of the Old Testament, from the conquest of the Promised Land to the exile. The remaining twenty-five lessons cover the life, death, and resurrection of Jesus in the New Testament gospels.

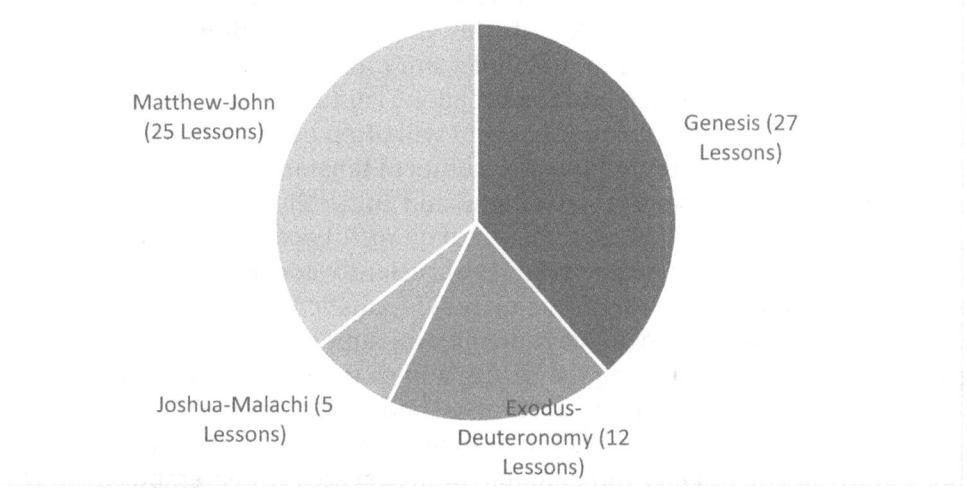

Figure 6.1: Biblical Distribution of McIlwain's Phase 1 Lessons

The visual depiction of McIlwain's selected portions of Scripture in figure 6.1 demonstrates how the very selection of which stories to tell in an oral curriculum is culturally informed. Thus, the importance of the worldview-based approach to biblical storytelling advocated by Tom Steffen and developed in-depth by Mike Matthews comes into view. To tailor the curriculum to the Inuit worldview, we must identify the topics that are relevant to them as revealed in

---

[411] McIlwain, 159.

their own oral traditions. What key cosmological questions are asked and answered in Inuit stories, and what does Scripture have to say about these same questions?

Adopting Matthew's terminology as established in chapter 2, three "Key Stories" emerge across Inuit culture from the ethnology developed in chapter 5.[412] In keeping with the relational emphasis of the present study, each can be described as a relational dyad: (1) the story of humans' relationship with the supernatural realm, (2) the story of humans' relationship with one another, and (3) the story of humans' relationship with the environment. This is certainly not an exhaustive list, and other key stories can be traced across the varied landscape of Inuit oral traditions. However, when viewed through the relational lens employed in the present study, these take prominence. These Key Stories emerge from countless individual "episodes" (specific oral traditions) from Inuit communities across the Arctic and are evident in the ethnology presented earlier. Together, they contribute to the "Master" Inuit story of what it means to be an *Inuk* (a real person), and this master story finds its place in the "Greatest Story"—the great metanarrative of the Triune God from eternity to eternity.

Having identified these three key stories, the task of the Bible teacher—and the future ministry leader—is to "tell God's story in light of their story," or to "restory" the Inuit experience into the broader Trinitarian metanarrative.[413] The two will not always be compatible, and will often be at odds with one another, but without understanding the points of tension, it is not possible to teach the biblical narrative in a meaningful and culturally relevant manner.

Returning to the Firm Foundations curriculum, it becomes evident that McIlwain's selection of biblical narratives sufficiently addresses only one of these three key stories. Writing from an individualistic Western perspective, McIlwain takes great care to address the human-supernatural story. He spends a great deal of time establishing the nature and character of God and the origin and fall of human beings, with most emphasis placed on themes of guilt and innocence. He also makes a special point to address the identity and role of supernatural spirits (angels and demons) in the created order, emphasizing that as created beings they have no authority over people. Since this is his chief concern, McIlwain is able to address these matters primarily within the Pentateuch and then move on to the life of Christ.

This approach fails to address the other two key stories that are of concern to the Inuit people. The Inuit do not think only in terms of the individual, but as a community. Personal vindication is rarely a major theme in their oral traditions—rather, human behavior is evaluated according to its influence on

---

[412] Matthews defines a "Key Story" as "a cluster of like-minded episodes that has gained prominence and power because of its embeddedness in a social group." Matthews, 91.
[413] Matthews, 209.

the community or kinship group. Moreover, of equal importance is the human relationship to the land and the sea, upon which the Inuit rely. As discussed previously, the environment is not seen as an impersonal force to be mastered, but a relationship that must be respected and cultivated to ensure continued survival. A Western reader might argue that these key stories should be excluded from the metanarrative altogether, wondering, "What do these themes have to do with personal salvation?" This, however, is the very line of thought that Matthews and Steffen caution us to avoid.

Unsurprisingly, a thorough reading of Scripture reveals much attention to both of these themes, and they are key aspects of the grand story of redemption. Men and women were created not only for personal relationship with God, but for one another (Gen. 1:27, 2:18), and were placed in an environment designed specifically to meet their needs (Gen. 1:28-30). Sin did not only separate humans from a Holy God, as McIlwain emphasizes so well. It also broke human relationships with one another (Gen. 3:16) and humanity's relationship with the environment (Gen. 3:17-19). All three themes are introduced in the creation account, impacted by the fall, and addressed in the story of redemption and reconciliation. To tell God's story in light of the Inuit story, McIlwain's exposition of Scripture must be expanded to make room for these themes.

Proposed Adjustments to Firm Foundations Phase 1

In telling the biblical story from an individualistic Guilt/Innocence framework, the most dominant Old Testament theme that McIlwain draws upon is that of "Law." To this end, two lessons are devoted to the Decalogue, and all but five of the Old Testament lessons are based on the Book of the Law. Though the law does have much to say about human relationships as well as the Israelites' relationship to the Promised Land, these remain underdeveloped. If we wish to include God's plan for human relationships and for the environment in the metanarrative of redemption, then it is necessary to shift this focus from the theme of "Law" to the theme of "Kingdom."[414]

The theme of Kingdom incorporates all three relational dimensions, as Scripture traces the unfolding plan of the sovereign Creator to restore Creation to submission to His rightful reign. To do this, He takes steps to reconcile humans not only to Himself, but also to one another and to the created order. He chooses one family—Israel—to model these restored relationships to the rest of the world, and gives them a land. With this land grant comes His law, functioning as a constitution governing their right to dwell in His land. In these themes of community and land, the Inuit can find much that resonates with

---

[414] I (John) am indebted to Scott Keen of Ethnos360 for this insight, which he suggested to me in personal conversation at the 2020 meeting of the Evangelical Missiological Society.

their own identity as a close-knit community of people working together for mutual survival in a land that ultimately belongs to their Creator.

Unfortunately, these themes are just getting started when McIlwain begins to "fast forward" through most of the Old Testament in Lesson 41. To develop a more complete understanding of God's Kingdom plan as it unfolds in the Old Testament, including His concern for human relationships and their impact upon the land, distinct lessons can be inserted into the curriculum chronologically based on the following passages.

Leviticus 24-25: The Law and the Land

This lesson establishes the correlation between the Mosaic Law and the Israelites' life in in Promised Land. It provides opportunities for reflection on Inuit traditions and taboos related to their own use of the land, emphasizing that the earth belongs to God, and that human actions do indeed have ramifications for the land in which they live. This chapter also brings some balance to McIlwain's emphasis on personal guilt and innocence in his treatment of the law from lessons 35 and 36 (the Ten Commandments). It is suggested that Lessons 35 & 36 be merged into a single lesson that can be complemented by this lesson.

Judges 19-21: The Levite and His Concubine

This lesson provides important perspective on life in the Promised Land apart from godly leadership. Emphasis is placed on the fact that "there was no king in Israel, and everyone did what was right in his own eyes." This led to rampant societal breakdown and dysfunction in family relationships. Shame is a major theme in this pericope, as the narrative itself does not focus on the guilt of the people, but rather the shame that was brought by their actions. Where appropriate, parallels may carefully be drawn to the breakdown in Inuit society after Western colonization and the introduction of alcohol. The Israelites failed to uphold God's law in His land, making the case for God to appoint a human king as His representative on earth. This lesson should replace the second half of Lesson 41, which covers a broad sweep from Numbers 27 to 1 Samuel 11. With the insertion of this lesson, Lesson 41 can be revised to focus on Joshua and the settlement of the Promised Land.

2 Samuel 11-12: David and Bathsheba

McIlwain treats the entire narratives of both David and Solomon in Lesson 42. Since these individuals play so heavily into the Kingdom theme and the Israelites' growing expectations for God's restoration of the entire created order, this lesson should be broken into several distinct lessons. Thus, the existing Lesson 42 will focus only on the anointing of David and importantly, the Davidic Covenant. This new lesson from 2 Samuel 11-12 provides an important complement to that lesson, emphasizing that even David was marred by the human condition. The narrative on David and Bathsheba emphasizes that even under godly human leadership, human relationships continued to suffer against God's intended design. Nevertheless, David's confession and repentance, and God's subsequent forgiveness, set an important precedent that provides hope for reconciliation.

1 Kings 10-11: Solomon

McIlwain treats Solomon in Lesson 42, but focuses only on his role in building the temple. Devoting an entire lesson to David's heir provides an opportunity to emphasize how close Solomon came to fulfilling the Messianic expectations, as the temple was built and news of God's honor spread to distant nations, before ultimately falling far short. Solomon's amassing of silver and gold, import of horses from Egypt, and multiplication of foreign wives in these chapters can be directly compared to the Mosaic Law of Deuteronomy 17:16-17, which prohibited the king from these exact activities. Thus, the search for the rightful heir to God's promise in 2 Samuel 7 continues.

1 Kings 12: God's Kingdom Divides

The division of the Kingdom of Israel has important bearing on the themes of both human society and land, emphasizing once again God's sovereignty in the affairs of humans and His divine purposes in the allotment of the nations of the earth. As land use continues to be a hot-button issue in contemporary debates between the Inuit and the governments of their colonizers, this narrative provides an opportunity to emphasize that though human arguments about land and territory are not God's design, He can use them for His good purposes, and He does not forget His people or promises. God's loyalty to the house of David further emphasizes the hope that the land will one day be healed.

1 Kings 16:29-27:1: The Sin of Ahab

The Ahab narrative is paradigmatic for many of the Israelite kings, all of whom failed to uphold God's law perfectly and none of whom filled the shoes of David. Notably, during Ahab's reign, we begin to see how human abuse of power directly results in drought and famine, just as predicted in Leviticus 25.

1 Kings 18: Elijah on Mt. Carmel

The Elijah narrative reminds us that as God's people continued to go their own way, He never left them without a witness. Furthermore, it provides an important comparison between the worshippers of God and the pagan priests of Baal. God's power over nature is emphasized, and human attempts to entreat spirits in order to influence the natural world are put in perspective. This narrative provides another opportunity to critically evaluate traditional practices meant to ensure successful hunting and harvest, and to "restory" such ideas into the biblical narrative of God's sovereignty over nature.

1 Kings 21: Ahab's Repentance

The story of Naboth's vineyard emphasizes continued breakdown in human relationships, while Ahab's act of repentance underscores the universal availability of God's grace. God's vow to put an end to Ahab's dynasty sets the trajectory for the Assyrian and Babylonian invasions that loom on the horizon.

Jeremiah 33, Ezekiel 31: New Covenant

The New Covenant is an important element of the scriptural metanarrative when viewed from a relational perspective. The ministries of Jeremiah and Ezekiel both drive home the point that God's people were unable to maintain the requirements of God's Law, and therefore would be banished from the land and from His presence. Nevertheless, God points ahead to a future restoration in which all three relational dimensions will be healed under the rightful heir to David's throne: human relationships will be set right (Ezekiel 34:20-24), the earth will provide for God's people (Ezekiel 34:24-29), and God will live with them as their shepherd (Ezekiel 34:30-31). This will be accomplished by God placing His Spirit within His people (Ezekiel 36:27) and writing His law upon their hearts (Jeremiah 31:33), allowing them to keep His commandments through a changed relational identity.

Jeremiah 52: The Fall of Jerusalem

In this narrative, the shame of the Israelites reaches its zenith as the consequences for neglecting God's law that were spelled out in Leviticus 25 reach their final fulfillment. The words of Jeremiah as he laments the city's fall emphasize not the personal feelings of guilt, but the societal shame that the nation experienced being banished from God's presence. This is an important point of emphasis considering the Inuit key story of human relationships, and the cultural orientation towards shame and honor. There are also important ramifications regarding the relationship to the land, which Israel lost. Important analogies may be drawn to the Inuit experience of losing rights and territory to their colonizers, which may in turn lead to greater appreciation for God's promises to heal the land and restore all of creation in His future kingdom.

Ezra 1, 6: The Jews Return and Rebuild the Temple

The Jewish return from captivity is an important "seed" that leads to the birth of Jesus and emphasizes that God's promises are not forgotten. By devoting an entire lesson to the story of Israel's return, more emphasis can be placed on the redemptive trajectory that is being set. The reconstruction of the temple has important ramifications for the theme of God's relationship to His people, and it is notable that His presence is not observed filling the temple in Ezra 6 like it did in 1 Kings 8. This emphasizes that though the people did return, God's promises were not completely fulfilled. The Jews—and the nations with them, including the Inuit—continue to wait for the restoration of relationships and the healing of the land that He promised. McIlwain treats this as part of his Lesson 45, which discusses the invasion, fall, captivity, and return in a single lesson. In light of the more detailed presentation of these stories as proposed here, Lesson 45 can be removed and replaced.

Pedagogical Note on Using the Firm Foundations Curriculum

It should be noted that the additional lessons suggested above do not follow the format used by McIlwain in his written curriculum. Rather than providing a systematic, point-by-point outline, my intention has been to emphasize only the general theme of selected narratives along with key emphases, allowing the presenter to take a true "storytelling" approach that will be more consistent with Inuit learning preferences. Though they are arranged chronologically to emphasize the unfolding narrative of Scripture at the big-picture level, McIlwain presents the information in point-by-point format, leading students through analytical theological truths as they emerge in the narrative. The lessons as structured by McIlwain are still better suited to expositional teaching in a classroom environment.

Consistent with the pedagogical observations made in the first section of this chapter, teachers using the Firm Foundations curriculum in Inuit contexts should consider using the written curriculum only as a general guide, and rely on the scriptural narrative itself, rather than propositional statements about the narrative, to convey the desired message. In other words, I suggest that teachers depart from McIlwain's analytical outlines and simply teach the stories from Scripture. Steffen and Bjoraker provide an appropriate model for this type of "oral hermeneutics" that can be employed.[415]

Summary

In this chapter, we have applied narrative logic and orality theory to the question of relational Inuit leadership development. Using Thigpen's theory of Learning Quadrants to classify different approaches to learning, we identified the Inuit as having a "Primary Orality" culture. This suggests that both pedagogical methods and curricular design must be adapted for effective ministry leadership development. In terms of pedagogy, the locus of trust in the learning process is not in vetted and credentialed authorities, but in human

---

[415] Tom Steffen and William Bjoraker, *The Return of Oral Hermeneutics: As Good Today as it Was for the Hebrew Bible and First-Century Christianity* (Eugene: Wipf & Stock, 2020).

relationships. This observation reinforced the relational emphasis presented in the previous chapter and led to the recommendation of several specific pedagogical tools to reorient learning activities in the classroom towards orality. In terms of curricular design, Firm Foundations was identified as an existing narrative-based curriculum that is already in use by various ministries serving Inuit people. We examined the first phase of this series from the perspective of "worldview-based storying" proposed by Tom Steffen and Mike Matthews. As its emphases were compared with key stories in the Inuit worldview, several deficiencies were noted, and eleven new lessons were proposed to better contextualize the curriculum to the Inuit worldview. This revised approach is not intended to represent a complete ministry leadership development program. Rather, it provides a curricular starting point for regular discipleship between the pastor or missionary and the disciple, and demonstrates how additional tools can be adapted for the process over the long term.

Table 6.1: Orality-based Model for Inuit Leadership Development

Orality-based Pedagogy		Narrative-based Curriculum	
Instruction (Transmission of content)	Audio-visual media Group Discussion Storytelling	**Inuit Key Stories**	Human-to-God Human-to-Human Human-to-Environment
Evaluation (Synthesis and retransmission of content)	Oral exams Oral presentations Group assignments Peer evaluation Inuit dancing	**Scriptural Metanarrative**	Creation Fall Reconciliation Restoration

Chapter 7
An Integrated Model for Inuit Ministry Leadership Development

A popular proverb observes, "It takes a village to raise a child," and this proverb could apply just as easily to ministry leadership development in Inuit contexts: "It takes a village to develop a leader." We have argued that a contextualized approach to developing Inuit leaders for ministry is dependent upon a wide network of relationships that contribute to the growth and development of an individual disciple. Building on the key relationships in the leadership development process, our model outlines how an individual pastor or missionary can form a small "school" of discipleship that revolves around regular mentoring in a small group environment. In addition to these regular small group activities, the model incorporates input from ministry partners to address areas that cannot necessarily be met at the local level, including vocational training, theological education modules, and trauma healing workshops. Within these various teaching contexts, from the small-group mentoring meetings to the regional modules, oral pedagogical methods are prescribed as the preferred means of learning, and a narrative-based approach to Bible study forms the curricular backbone for the regular small-group discipleship meetings led by the pastor or missionary. Table 7.1 summarizes the key aspects and objectives of this integrated model.

Table 7.1: Integrated Model for Inuit Ministry Leadership Development

Frequency	Discipleship Activity	Relational Emphasis	Oral Methodology	Competency Objective
Regular (Daily, or multiple times per week)	Prayer and Bible study	God	Group prayer, recorded Scripture, Bible storying	Character transformation
	Small group mentoring	Pastor/Missionary Mentor	Group discussion, Bible storying	Understanding of scriptural metanarrative
	Ministry modeling	Pastor/Missionary Mentor	Demonstration, observation, apprenticeship	Understanding of leadership responsibilities
	Job skills development[416]	Community	Demonstration, observation, apprenticeship	Ability to support ministry bi-vocationally
Frequently (Weekly, or multiple times per month)	Environmental excursions	Environment	Object lessons, modeling	Environmental respect for sustainable ministry
	Local Visitation	Elders, Family, Community	Discussion, storytelling, observation	Demonstrate care for community and honor for elders
	Ministry Duties	Congregation	Hands-on experimentation	Ability to teach and lead in congregational setting
Occasionally (Quarterly or annually)	Theological Education Modules	Instructor	Oral instruction & assessment	Intellectual understanding of key theological principles
	Trauma Healing & Recovery Workshops	Community; demonic realm	Group sharing, art-based reflection	Dealing with shame; resisting spiritual oppression; overcoming addiction
	Hosting mature Christian elders	Elders	Discussion, LLDM[417]	Character transformation

---

[416] The frequency and nature of this aspect will vary based on the local economy.
[417] Mikeska, 6.

This is not intended as a comprehensive training curriculum to be implemented indiscriminately. Rather, it is an alternative model—a new way of thinking about how indigenous leaders can be identified, developed, and accepted through a relational, orality-based process. The goal is that this model can be adopted—and, crucially, *adapted*—by churches and ministries serving all Inuit communities with a view towards instilling contextualized, culturally-relevant leadership values in the church.

Moreover, this model is not meant to replace any ministries already in operation. Rather, our vision is that it will "connect the dots" between pastors and missionaries serving individual communities, and regional programs such as theological education modules, vocational training, and counseling ministries that can support them in the process. All of the pieces for this model are already in operation right now; they merely need to be assembled. In order for this to take place, regional denominations and mission agencies should consider appointing a specific person to serve as a catalyst and shepherd who can guide local pastors and missionaries towards this goal. This person will support training efforts at the local level by coordinating resources and building a regional support network for leadership development.

Recommendations for Further Study

Of course, the task is not complete, and over the course of this study a number of areas have emerged which merit further research that will carry forward the discussion on Inuit leadership development. From a historical perspective, this study was limited in scope to Evangelical ministries. As noted in several instances, non-Evangelical branches of Christianity have also established ministries among the Inuit, including the Roman Catholic, Anglican, and Lutheran churches. Pentecostal churches, too, have found success ministering among the Inuit, some of which do identify as Evangelical. This study included a discussion of the Pentecostal INO churches of Greenland within its scope, but more can be learned by researching the methods used by non-Evangelical groups.

From an anthropological perspective, this study focused on the areas of education, leadership, and social control because of their central roles in the question of ministry leadership development. By studying these three areas alone, three key stories emerged that informed the task of curriculum development. A broader study of Inuit oral traditions would undoubtedly yield further insights that can be incorporated into a worldview-based storying curriculum.

In terms of curriculum, ethnohermeneutics is an emerging field of missiological interest not broached by this study, apart from the brief appeal to reconsider how Bible study methods are addressed in a narrative-based curriculum. The description of an Inuit hermeneutic could be an entire research project in itself, and would lend important insights to all involved in the leadership development process.

Another important curricular endeavor that remains is to contextualize the remaining phases of the Firm Foundations curriculum for an Inuit audience, as this study has demonstrated with the first phase. Alternatively, a completely new narrative-based curriculum, developed from the ground up from a worldview-based perspective, would not be out of the question.

Broader Missiological Implications

Some of these insights from the Inuit context may be relevant to the broader question of ministry leadership development around the world. By remapping the relational dyads surrounding the question of leadership development to other societies, the relational model that we propose could be applied in other contexts. Our application of Honor/Shame theory to the question of theological education may be useful to institutions serving other cultures in which honor and shame are emphasized in social control. In the same way, institutions serving other "primary orality" cultures may be able to apply some of the same pedagogical principles suggested in chapter 6. Even in Western contexts, institutions of theological education may find some helpful insights as younger generations are observed moving towards secondary orality as a learning preference, towards honor and shame as a framework for social control, and towards relationality as a correction against the impersonal and dehumanizing engine of globalization. There is certainly much more work to be done. It will take a village. May each ministry represented in this paper, and many more around the globe, continue to find its place in the task.

Appendix 1
Research Design: Data Collection and Data Analysis

This book began as a doctoral dissertation written by John Ferch, with Enoch Wan serving as First Reader. Dr. Gary Ridley of SEND International served as the Second Reader. For those interested, the detailed research design that guided this dissertation is provided here:

This study aimed to develop a model integrating relational and narrative logic for ministry leadership development that is glocalized to Inuit contexts. It followed a specific plan informed by established research procedures, as follows.

Methodological Design

This was a qualitative research project that employed ethnography to develop a culturally-relevant model for ministry leadership development among circumpolar Inuit people groups. Since the study aimed to compare cultural perspectives on leadership across a wide swath of related people groups, rather than to zero in on one particular community, it employed ethnology, rather than the more common techniques of participant observation or interviews, for the collection and analysis of data.

Research Process & Procedures

Having selected ethnology as an appropriate research tool for the project at hand, the first step in the research was to identify a sufficient body of ethnographic literature pertaining to circumpolar Inuit communities. The second step was a historical overview of existing leadership development programs serving Inuit communities.

Upon identifying the necessary ethnographic literature and ministry programs currently providing ministry leadership development, the data analysis step was able to begin. This step is described in detail below, under "Technique." Due to the ongoing, iterative nature of ethnographic research, data analysis proceeded concurrently with data collection. Data from ethnographic literature and the sample leadership development programs was coded according to the various theoretical paradigms that emerged from the literature review, allowing recurring themes and trends to emerge. These were then interpreted to develop a contextualized model for Inuit leadership development, which is presented as the final step of the research.

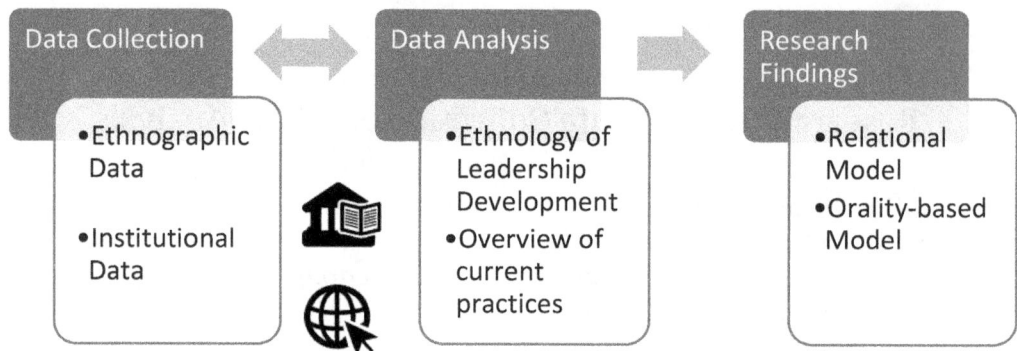

Figure A1.1: Research Design

Technique

Data collection proceeded in two stages, both of which were predominantly archival in nature. First, I collected a sufficient body of ethnographic literature pertaining to circumpolar Inuit culture, focusing on formally-published primary source material and academic studies. In the second phase, I gathered information on existing ministry leadership development programs serving Inuit people. Since formally-published literature on these programs tends to be scant (with the exception of historical literature which will be identified in Phase 1), I relied on web searches and personal correspondence to locate relevant data from the various institutions (including academic catalogs, websites, and promotional material). Where appropriate and necessary, I supplemented this material with informal interviews with institutional leaders conducted through email and phone calls.

Summary

This study was conducted using ethnological analysis of existing ethnographic and educational data pertaining to Inuit communities and the ministry leadership development programs that are serving them. Application of relational and narrative logic to this data allowed the development of a glocally-contextualized model for Inuit ministry leadership development.

Bibliography

Alaska Bible College Academic Catalog 2017-2018 (Palmer: Alaska Bible College, 2017).

Alaska Bible Seminary Student Handbook. Bethel: Alaska Bible Seminary, 2015.

Alaska Christian College Academic Catalog 2020-2021 (Soldotna: Alaska Christian College, 2020).

Alaska Natives Commission/Alaska Federation of Natives. "Alaska Native Education: Report of the Education Task Force." In *Alaska Native Education: Views from Within*. Fairbanks: Alaska Native Knowledge Network, 2013.

Almquist, L. Arden. *Covenant Missions in Alaska.* Chicago: Covenant, 1962.

Assembly of Alaska Native Educators. *Alaska Standards for Culturally-Responsive Schools.* Fairbanks: Alaska Native Knowledge Network, 1998.

Bailey, Garrick & James Peoples. *Introduction to Cultural Anthropology.* Belmont: Wadsworth, 1999.

Barnhardt, Ray & Angayuqaq Oscar Kawagley. "Culture, Chaos, and Complexity." In *Alaska Native Education: Views from Within.* Fairbanks: Alaska Native Knowledge Network, 2010.

Bates, Clifton & Michael J. Oleksa. *Conflicting Landscapes: American Schooling/Alaska Natives.* Anchorage: Kuskokwim Corporation, 2007.

Bechtel, Jason. "Moving into Northern Canada." *NTM@work*, June 2017. https://ethnos.ca/moving-into-northern-canada/.

Caldwell, Larry. "Theological Institutions and Orality: Paying Attention to Non-readers at Home and Abroad." Conference presentation at Evangelical Missiological Society Annual Meeting, Dallas, TX, October 9, 2020. https://youtu.be/-5Q1Fytw5bk.

Casey, Anthony (ed.). *Iqaluit Ethnography.* Unpublished missiological ethnography, North American Mission Board, 2009.

Chance, Norman. *The Eskimo of North Alaska.* New York: Holt, Rinehart, and Winston, 1966.

Cochran, Rosie. *Founded: The Heritage of Ethnos360.* Sanford: Ethnos360, 2017.

Collier, John, Jr. *Alaskan Eskimo Education: A Film Analysis of Cultural Confrontation in the Schools.* San Francisco: Holt, Rinehart, & Winston, 1973.

Conchran, Patricia A. L., Catherine A. Marshall, Carmen Garcia-Downing, Elizabeth Kendall, Doris Cook, Laurie McCubbin, & Reva Mariah S. Gover. "Indigenous Ways of Knowing: Implications for Participatory Research and Community." *American Journal of Public Health.* Vol. 98, no. 1 (January 2008). 22-27.

Crandall, Faye. *Into the Copper River Valley: The Letters and Ministry of Vincent James Joy, Pioneer Missionary to Alaska.* Taylors: Faith, 1994.

Darnell, Frank & Anton Hoëm. *Taken to Extremes: Education in the Far North.* Oslo: Scandinavian University, 1996.

Department of Education, Culture, and Employment. *Inuuqatigiit: The Curriculum from the Inuit Perspective.* Yellowknife: Northwest Territories, 1996.

Duffy, R. Quinn. "Providing an Education." *The Road to Nunavut: The Progress of the Eastern Arctic Inuit since the Second World War.* Montreal: McGill-Queen's University, 1988.

Durkalec, Agata. *Inuit Nunaat: Inuit Homeland.* Scale 1:9,000,000. Ottawa: Inuit Circumpolar Council, 2017.

Eastty, Michelle. "Ferches join faculty." *NorthWord: A Publication of Alaska Bible College* (Summer 2012).

"Eastward Expansion." *SEND North: Making Northern Disciple-makers* (Winter 2018). 1.

Egede, Ingmar. "Educational Problems in Greenland." *Pedagogik.* Vol. 6, no. 2 (May 1976).

Ferch, Gary & Donna. "Greenland." *Brown Gold* (February 1990).

Ferris, Robert. "Leadership Development in Missions Settings." *Missiology: An Introduction to the Foundations, History, and Strategies of World Missions.* Nashville: B&H, 2015. 457-470.

Fienup-Riordan, Ann. *Boundaries and Passages: Rule and Ritual in Yup'ik Eskimo Oral Tradition.* Norman: University of Oklahoma, 1994.

———. *The Nelson Island Eskimo: Social Structure and Ritual Distribution.* Anchorage: Alaska Pacific University, 1983.

———. *Qaluyaarmiuni Nunamtenek Qanemciput: Our Nelson Island Stories.* Anchorage: Calista Elders Council, 2011.

Flemming, Isabelle M. "Ethnography and Ethnology." *21st Century Anthropology: A Reference Handbook.* Vol. 1. Los Angeles: SAGE, 2010. 153-161.

"Frikirke-fusion på vej i Grønland." *Kristeligt Dagblad*, 4 September 1999. https://www.kristeligt-dagblad.dk/kirke-tro/frikirke-fusion-p%C3%A5-vej-i-gr%C3%B8nland (Accessed 8 September 2020).

Furman, Clarence "Barney." *Serving by God's Power in the North.* Pre-release copy. Boring: InterAct, 2017.

Georges, Jayson & Mark D. Baker. *Ministering in Honor-Shame Cultures.* Downers Grove: InterVarsity, 2016.

Georges, Jayson. *The 3D Gospel.* N.p.: Time, 2014.

Grunlan, Stephen A. & Marvin K. Mayers. *Cultural Anthropology: A Christian Perspective.* Grand Rapids: Zondervan, 1979.

Hanson, Douglas. "Preparing Melanesians for Missions." *Transforming Teaching for Mission: Educational Theory and Practice.* Wilmore: First Fruits, 2014. 247-263.

Henkelman, James W. & Kurt H. Vitt. *Harmonious to Dwell: The History of the Alaska Moravian Church, 1885-1985.* Bethel: Tundra, 1985.

Hiebert, Paul G. *Missiological Implications of Epistemological Shifts: Affirming Truth in a Modern/Postmodern World.* Harrisburg: Trinity, 1999.

———. *Transforming Worldviews: An Anthropological Understanding of How People Change.* Grand Rapids: Baker, 2008.

Hild, Carl. "Alaska Native Traditional Knowledge and Ways of Knowing." In *Alaska Native Education: Views from Within.* Fairbanks: Alaska Native Knowledge Network, 2010.

Holtved, Erik. "Eskimo Shamanism." *Scripta Instituti Donneriani Aboensis.* Vol. 1 (August 1967). 23-31.

Hoppe, Michael H. "Crosscultural Issues in Leadership Development." *The Center for Creative Leadership Handbook of Leadership Development.* Ed. Cynthia D. McCaulley, Russ S. Moxley, and Ellen Van Velsor. San Francisco: Jossey Bass, 1998.

Huntington, Mary. "Saturday PM Session." Conference presentation at Would Jesus Eat Frybread?, Anchorage, AK, November 11, 2017. https://youtu.be/HjFlh05omBI?t=1811.

InterAct Ministries Member Handbook. Boring: InterAct Ministries, 2007.

Johnson, R. Burke & Larry Christensen. *Educational Research: Quantitative, Qualitative, and Mixed Approaches.* 6th ed. Los Angeles: Sage, 2017.

Jones-Sparck, Lucy. "Effects of Modernization on the Cup'ik of Alaska." In *Alaska Native Education: Views from Within.* Fairbanks: Alaska Native Knowledge Network, 2010.

Jorgenson, Larry. "From Shamans to Missionaries: The Popular Religiosity of the Inupiaq Eskimo." *Word & World* vol. 10, no. 4, 339-348.

Kawagaley, Angayuqaq Oscar, Delena Norris-Tull, & Roger Norris-Tull. "The Indigenous Worldview of Yupiaq Culture: Its Scientific Nature and Relevance to the Practice and Teaching of Science." In *Alaska Native Education: Views from Within.* Fairbanks: Alaska Native Knowledge Network, 2010.

Kawagaley, Angayuqaq Oscar. "Alaska Native Education: History and Adaptation in the New Millenium." In *Alaska Native Education: Views from Within.* Fairbanks: Alaska Native Knowledge Network, 2010.

Kelling, Fred. *Fisherman of Faroe: William Gibson Sloan.* Gota: Leirkerid, 1993.

Kleinfeld, Judith. *Effective Teachers of Indian and Eskimo High School Students.* Fairbanks: Institute of Social, Economic and Government Research, 1972.

———. "Intellectual Strengths in Culturally Different Groups: An Eskimo Illustration." *Review of Educational Research.* Vol. 43, no. 3 (September 1973). 341-359.

Langdon, Steve J. *The Native People of Alaska: Traditional Living in a Northern Land.* Anchorage: Greatland, 2002.

Lantis, Margaret. *The Social Culture of the Nunivak Eskimo.* Philadelphia: American Philosophical Society, 1946.

Laugrand, Frédéric B. & Jarich G. Oosten. *Inuit Shamanism and Christianity: Transitions and Transformation in the Twentieth Century.* Montreal: McGill-Queen's, 2010.

Lazell, J. Arthur. *Alaskan Apostle: The Life Story of Sheldon Jackson.* New York: Harper & Brothers, 1960.

Ledyard, Gleason H. *And to the Eskimos.* Chicago: Moody, 1958.

Ledyard, Gleason & Kathryn. "Introduction." *Holy Bible - Old and New Testaments: New Life Version.* Uhrichsville: Barbour, 2014.

Malvich, Eva. "Native Missionaries in Rural Alaska." *Friends of Covenant History* (Summer/Fall 2015). 7.

Mathiassen, Therkel. "Ethnology of the Greenland Eskimos." *Encylopedia Arctica.* Vol. 8. Washington: Office of Naval Research, 1951.

Matthews, Michael. *A Novel Approach: The Significance of Story in Interpreting Reality.* Victoria: Tellwell, 2017.

McGregor, Heather E. *Inuit Education and Schools in the Eastern Arctic.* Vancouver: UBC, 2010.

McIlwain, Trevor. *Building on Firm Foundations: Guidelines for Evangelism & Teaching Believers.* Revised Edition. Sanford: New Tribes Mission, 2005.

Mezirow, Jack. "Learning to Think Like an Adult: Core Concepts of Transformation Theory." In *Learning as Transformation: Critical Perspectives on a Theory in Progress.* San Francisco: Jossey-Bass, 2000.

Mikeska, Shane. *Engaging the Secular World through Life-on-Life Disciple-making in The British Context.* DIS product, Western Seminary, 2017.

More, Arthur J. "Learning Styles and Indian Students: A Review of Research." Paper presented at the Mokakit Indian Education Research Conference. London, Ontario, Canada, July 25-27, 1984.

Muller, Roland. *Honor & Shame: Unlocking the Door.* Bloomington: Xlibris, 2000.

Napoleon, Harold. *Yuuyaraq: The Way of the Human Being.* Fairbanks: Alaska Native Knowledge Network, 1996.

Naske, Claus M. & Herman E. Slotnick. *Alaska: A History.* 3rd ed. Norman: University of Oklahoma, 2011.

Neill, Stephen. *A History of Christian Missions.* 2nd ed. London: Penguin, 1986.

Okakok, Leona. "Serving the Purpose of Education." In *Alaska Native Education: Views from Within.* Fairbanks: Alaska Native Knowledge Network, 2013.

Oleksa, Michael & Richard Dauenhauer. "Education in Russian America." In *Education in Alaska's Past.* Anchorage: Alaska Historical Society, 1982.

Pete, Cynthia. *A Native Tradition and Christianity.* B.A. product, Alaska Bible College, 2015.

Plueddemann, James E. *Leading Across Cultures: Effective Ministry and Mission in the Global Church.* Downers Grove: InterVarsity, 2009.

Preston, Jane P.; Claypool, Tim R.; Rowluck, William; and Green, Brenda. "Exploring the Concepts of Traditional Inuit Leadership and Effective School Leadership in Nunavut (Canada)." *Comparative and International Education / Éducation Comparée et Internationale* vol. 44, iss. 2, article 2 (2015).

Rasmussen, Knud. *The Netsilik Eskimos: Social Life and Spiritual Culture.* Vol. 8 (1-2) of *Report of the Fifth Thule Expedition 1921-24.* Copenhagen: Gyldendalske Boghandel, 1931.

Ray, Dorothy Jean. *The Eskimos of Bering Strait, 1650-1898.* Seattle: University of Washington, 1975.

Rempel, Barry James. *An Action Research Exploration of Leadership Formation Among the Ahtna That Resulted in the Discovery of Factors Encouraging the Emergence of Indigenous Christian Leaders.* D.Min. product, Tyndale Seminary, 2014.

Ridley, Gary J. *Leadership Development in Native Alaskan Churches: Teaching Biblical Leadership Principles in the Light of an Analysis of Traditional Patterns of Leadership.* D.Miss. product, Trinity Evangelical Divinity School, 1990.

Roberts, Arthur O. *Tomorrow is Growing Old: Stories of the Quakers in Alaska.* Newberg: Barclay, 1978.

Savok, Fred. *Jesus and the Eskimo: How the Man of the Sky Brought the Light to My People.* Fairbanks: HLC, 2004.

Steffen, Tom. *The Facilitator Era: Beyond Pioneer Church Multiplication.* Eugene: Wipf & Stock, 2011.

———. *Worldview-based Storying: The Integration of Symbol, Story and Ritual in the Orality Movement.* Richmond: Orality Resources International, 2018.

Steffen, Tom & William Bjoraker. *The Return of Oral Hermeneutics: As Good Today as it Was for the Hebrew Bible and First-Century Christianity.* Eugene: Wipf & Stock, 2020.

Thigpen, Lynn. *Connected Learning: A Grounded Theory Study of how Cambodian Adults with Limited Formal Education Learn.* Ph.D. product, Biola University, 2016.

Thomas, Tay. *Cry in the Wilderness.* Anchorage: Color Art, 1967.

Tucker, Ruth. *From Jerusalem to Irian Jaya: A Biographial History of Christian Missions.* Grand Rapids: Zondervan, 1983.

Uhl-Bien, Mary. "Relational Leadership Theory: Exploring the Social Processes of Leadership and Organizing." *Leadership Quarterly* vol. 17 (2006), 654-676.

United Nations, General Assembly. *United Nations Declaration on the Rights of Indigenous Peoples.* A/61/L.67 (7 September 2007).

Untitled article. *NorthWord: A Publication of Alaska Bible College* (Fall 2010).

Wan, Enoch & Mark Hedinger. *Relational Missionary Training.* Skyforest: Urban Loft, 2017.

Wan, Enoch. "Diaspora Missiology and International Student Ministry." *Diaspora Missions to International Students.* Portland: Western Seminary, 2019. 11-42.

———. "The Paradigm of 'Relational Realism.'" *EMS Occasional Bulletin.* Vol. 19, no. 2 (Spring 2006), 1-4.

———. "Relational Theology and Relational Missiology." *EMS Occasional Bulletin.* Vol. 21, no. 1 (Fall 2007), 1-8.

Winter, Ralph and Bruce Koch. "Finishing the Task." *Perspectives on the World Christian Movement*, 4th edition. Pasedena: William Carey Library, 2009. 531-546.

Wright, Christopher. *The Mission of God.* Grand Rapids: InterVarsity, 2006.

Wright, N.T. *The New Testament and the People of God.* Minneapolis: Fortress, 1992.

www.ingramcontent.com/pod-product-compliance
Lightning Source LLC
Chambersburg PA
CBHW061328040426
42444CB00011B/2815